MINERAL KING

Southern Sequoia National Park & part of Golden Trout Wilderness

Ron Felzer

WILDERNESS PRESS
BERKELEY

Acknowledgements

I would like to thank each of the following for their help in updating and upgrading this edition of *Mineral King*: Kevin Stevens of Coalinga; Randy Coffman, J. Thomas Jeffrey, Colin Smith, Lorenzo Stowell and Tom Suk, all of the National Park Service; and Bill Deisman, of the U.S. Forest Service; and my sister Linda for her help with the photographs in this edition. Without their assistance and their knowledge-sharing about this area, this book would be incomplete and lacking in many ways. Tom Winnett continues to be a most understanding and keen editor of this series. Any errors or omissions that remain are solely my responsibility.

—Ron Felzer   *Richmond, California April 1992*

Copyright © 1972, 1981, 1992 by Ron Felzer
First edition May 1972
Second edition May 1981
THIRD EDITION May 1992
Second printing November 1996

Library of Congress Card Catalog Number 92-11415
International Standard Book Number 0-89997-122-9

Manufactured in the United States of America
Published by Wilderness Press
　　　　2440 Bancroft Way
　　　　Berkeley, CA 94704
　　　　(800) 443-7227   FAX (510) 548-1355

Write, call or fax for a free catalog

Library of Congress Cataloging-in Publication Data

Felzer, Ron.
　Mineral King / by Ron Felzer ; drawings by Marian Mayeda ; photos by the author. -- 3rd ed.
　　　p.　　cm. -- (High Sierra hiking guide)
　Includes bibliographical references (p.) and index.
　ISBN 0-89997-122-9
　1. Hiking--California--Mineral King Valley--Guidebooks.
2. Mineral King Valley (Calif.)--Guidebooks. I. Title.
II. Series: High Sierra hiking guide (1986)
GV199.42.C22M564 1992
917.94'86—dc20　　　　　　　　　　　　　　92-11415

Contents

Our Purpose

THE HIGH SIERRA HIKING GUIDES published by Wilderness Press are a set of pocket guides to the famous High Sierra. Each guide covers at least one 15-minute U.S. Geological Survey topographic quadrangle, an area about 14 miles east-west by 17 miles north-south. The first page shows the location of the area covered by this guide.

There is a great and increasing demand for literature about America's favorite wilderness, John Muir's "Range of Light." To meet this demand, we have undertaken this guide series. The purpose of each book in the series is threefold: first, to provide a reliable basis for planning a trip; second, to serve as a field guide while you are on the trail; and third, to stimulate you to further field investigation and background reading. Each guide describes a minimum of 100 miles of trails, and the descriptions are supplemented with a map and other logistical and background information. *High Sierra Hiking Guides* are based on first-hand observation. There is absolutely no substitute for walking the trails, so for this guide we walked and mapped all the trails.

In planning this series, we chose the 15-minute quadrangle as the unit because—though every way of dividing the Sierra is arbitrary—the 15-minute quadrangle map is the chosen aid of almost every wilderness traveler. Inside the back cover of this book is a map of the quadrangle, showing all described trails. With this map, you can always get where you want to go, with a minimum of detours or wasted effort.

The Country

The Great Western Divide cuts this land in two. Snaking north-south for 40 miles, this impressive granite ridge is the most prominent feature of the landscape in the *Mineral King* quadrangle.

To the west are the forks of the mighty Kaweah, rushing to the Central Valley. Separated from this river system by the Great Western Divide is an equally great stream, the south-flowing Kern River. Far below the peaks of the Divide toward the Pacific are long canyons bordered by stands of the earth's largest living things: *Sequoiadendron giganteum*: the big tree, or giant sequoia. Higher up these canyons and approaching the summit ridge itself are magnificent forests of pine and fir, and among them are pristine lakes and streams fed by deep winter snows. Above all tower the peaks of the Great Western Divide itself, raised from the bowels of the earth millions of years ago, later uplifted even higher, and then sculpted by glaciers several times. Up the slopes of these peaks forests give way to alpine meadows, and finally to talus slopes and sheer cliffs of granite, where only lichens and a few hardy forbs and grasses are able to subsist.

East of the Divide there are no sequoias. The climate is drier and colder. Here forests of foxtail and lodgepole pine grow where less frost-resistant and less drought-tolerant trees cannot make it. Pervading the scene, however, is a moonlike landscape: miles of bare granite ridges and plateaus straining high above green, **U**-shaped valleys.

Beyond the Great Western Divide, not much Central Valley smog ever penetrates to mar the scene, although it is common these days during late season in west-side canyons. The nights are crystalline, and the stars are still clearly visible to the night watcher.

The Divide is not only a barrier to plants and a modifier of climate, it is also a separator of people. Long approaches and steep, high passes keep most mountain visitors to *Mineral King* country down in the low west-slope forests. The stark and rugged granite land beyond the Divide to the east belongs only to those who earn its tranquility by spending many long, sweaty hours afoot. It is still today a remote and harshly beautiful land, much as it looked to those who first looked down upon it from the Great Western Divide.

Looking east from the outlet of Little Claire Lake

The History

Mineral King and Sequoia National Park history begins--as does history in the rest of the Sierra and of California--with native Californians, the Indians. Here the Shoshonean branch of the Uto-Aztecan language family was represented by the western Mono, or Monache, and Tubatulabal groups. These people in turn were related to the Owens Valley Paiutes who lived east of the Sierra and to the Hopis of Arizona.

Little is known of the earliest inhabitants of this area. It is believed that the Monache people living here at the time of the white man's arrival had crossed over the Sierra from the east only about 500 years before to take up residence in the drainage of the forks of the Kaweah River.

Hale D. Tharp, probably the first white man to see the Giant Forest, was asked by the Potwisha tribe of Monaches at Hospital Rock on the Middle Fork of the Kaweah to decipher the pictographs painted on the face of the rock. Naturally, Tharp didn't understand what these ancient rock writings had to say; but it is startling that the Indians living there didn't know either. This lends credence to the archaeological observation that different, prehistoric peoples inhabited the region before the people that met the first settlers arrived here.

Most of the evidence of Indian habitation in the *Mineral King* area is in the Giant Forest and at Kings Canyon. No clear evidence of Indian settlements exists at Mineral King itself, although there is a bedrock mortar site near Atwell Mill. However, such evidence as obsidian chippings at numerous lakes and trail campsites in the high country supports the contention that Indians used this area for summer hunting and for trade routes across the mountains to the land of the Paiutes in the east. With the settlers came disease and oppression. By 1865 smallpox, scarlet fever, measles and guns had killed off most of the Monaches in the Kaweah; the survivors fled east to the desert and disappeared.

Kaweah Peaks Ridge

The effects of the Gold Rush and the pressure for grazing land after the floods and drought of 1862-1864 opened up the southern Sierra for good. The green meadows of the high country were taken to be a commons to be exploited by all comers. Over-grazing was the inevitable result, and by 1873 what John Muir aptly referred to as "hooved locusts" had reduced the velvet meadows to a "gray sea of rolling granite ridges," in the words of Clarence King.

Mining here was not nearly as extensive or destructive as sheep-herding. While working for the Union Army as a meat-hunter with the construction crew of the Hockett Trail in 1864 Harry O'Farrell crossed over Farewell Gap from the south and probably was the first to see Mineral King. Here was a remote and beautiful valley teeming with game. He staked the first mining claim here in Monarch Canyon in 1872.

The next year, J.A. Crabtree, following an "Indian spirit," discovered a vein of ore and staked the White Chief claim. Mineral King Mining District was soon formed. Local newspapers downstream in Visalia and Porterville trumpeted the great discovery. The rush was on.

The summer of 1874 saw much hard labor and little result to show for it, but good advertising attracted money from the east. The New England Tunnel and Smelter Company showed up in 1875 and promptly bought up individual claims, paying in company stock. However, since the company was the chief purveyor of supplies at Mineral King, it soon had most of the stock back in the hands of its board of directors. These sharp-eyed engineers quickly realized that Mineral King was no Comstock Lode and after pronouncing the ore "rebellious," they pulled out in 1877.

One last flourish of activity occurred before mining in Mineral King effectively ended in 1881. Tom Fowler, a local boy, attracted some San Francisco capital and actually got a toll road, tramway, and smelter built. He reportedly carried the one silver ingot produced at the mill back and forth from the mill to the miners to encourage them in their fruitless toil. However, within two years, low-value ore and avalanches had convinced nearly everyone concerned that Mineral King was a bust, and mining ceased.

Meanwhile lumbering was having its effect on the giant sequoia groves downstream. By 1864 big trees in the Grant Grove (now part of Kings Canyon National Park) were being cut for fence posts, along with pine and fir for lumber. Actually, sequoia was not favored because of its size and its brittleness. Big trees were difficult to fell, and many broke apart upon hitting the ground. The construction of flumes in 1889 opened up country previously considered inaccessible, and loud voices soon were urging protection for the remaining magnificent groves in a national park.

Beginning as early as 1878 the Visalia *Delta*, under editor-publisher George A. Stewart, and local residents of Tulare County were petitioning Congress to set aside large areas of Sierra forests and high country permanently. However, it was not until September 25, 1890, that President Benjamin Harrison signed the bill setting aside two townships and four sections along the South Fork of the Kaweah as Sequoia National Park — "a pleasuring-ground for all the people." A week later Congress, surprisingly, created Yosemite National Park, increased the size of Sequoia and established General Grant Park all in one day!

Continuing agitation for the protection of complete watersheds bore fruit in February 1893, when President Benjamin Harrison established the Sierra Forest Reserve (under the act of March 1, 1891), encompassing 4 million acres of land from Yosemite to the southern Sierra. This vast forest reserve was later split into four national forests, Kings Canyon National Park, and additions to Sequoia National Park.

Mineral King became part of Sequoia National Forest in 1907, the year the "forest reserves" became "national forests." Though topographically and ecologically a part of Sequoia National Park, it was not included in the park because of the development and settlement that continued on there after the mining boom had ended.

By the 1930s a previously dreaded part of Mineral King's environment, snow, revealed itself as a new and positive attraction to the valley. Winters were mild, and the snowpack lasted till late spring. The Tulare County Board of Supervisors sponsored a snow survey of Mineral King in 1947 and recommended that the Valley be developed as a winter-sports area. The Forest Service and the Sierra Club concurred, and in 1949 the Forest Service invited proposals for the construction of recreational facilities at Mineral King.

Sixteen years later, in March of 1965, six developers' plans were tentatively okayed by the Forest Service, and more detailed information was requested before the final choice of a contractor would be made. In 1969 the choice had narrowed to two, and in July a three-member panel in Washington granted a permit to Disney Enterprises of Burbank, California, to build a year-round recreation complex in Mineral King. Then began nearly 10 years of court battles and legal maneuverings, after environmentalists, particularly the Sierra Club, realized what the proposed development would do to Mineral King.

At one time, the Disney plan envisioned a year-round alpine village complete with hotels, movie theaters, restaurants, cabins and ski lifts. On peak weekends there would have been 10,000 people on the valley floor. There would have been an immense impact on the air and water quality and on the scenery of Mineral King. The proposal was also opposed on several other grounds, such as violating Mineral King's status as a game refuge, dating from 1926, and allowing leases that exceeded the legal maximum for development on National Forest land.

The issue was finally resolved when the National Parks and Recreation Act of 1978 was signed by President Carter, adding Mineral King to Sequoia National Park. The Park Service's Comprehensive Management Plan, published in July 1980, basically envisions maintaining the area in its present condition, with little additional development. This proposal, when implemented, should help keep Mineral King in its mostly natural state for the foreseeable future and finally end the many years of contention and controversy swirling about this lovely subalpine valley.

The Geology

Millions of years of erosion by water, ice and snow working with gravity have sculpted the *Mineral King* landscape into the fantastic cliffs and canyons we see today.

Sedimentary strata laid down in seas over 200 million years ago and then invaded by molten magma from the bowels of the earth have been drastically altered from their original appearance and form by the action of erosive agents. Marine sediments of limestone, shale and sandstone which made up the ancestral Sierra Nevada were invaded from below by intrusions of granitic magma about 100 million years ago, in the Mesozoic era. Four periods of great uplifts during Cenozoic times created the Sierra fault block as we know it today — a mass of granite over 400 miles long and 40-80 miles wide. This block, or batholith, slopes gently toward the Central Valley in the west and steeply toward the Great Basin in the east.

With each period of uplift the cutting action for rivers was enhanced and gently graded valleys turned into steep, V-shaped canyons. These mountain-building episodes and consequent water erosion did not, however, erase all the old land surfaces; we can see, looking about the country described in this guide, that parts of these primeval landscapes are still visible.

In Mineral King valley, some of the most ancient sedimentary and volcanic rocks in the Sierra (since changed by heat and pressure into *metamorphic* rocks) are exposed as a remnant underlain and intruded by granitic magmas. From high passes on the Great Western Divide, hikers can see remnants of several early uplift surfaces in the extremely flat surfaces of Boreal Plateau, Chagoopa Plateau, and the top of Mount Whitney.

Although examples of early landforms can still be found in this country, they have been and are being constantly altered by erosion. Rivers like the Kern and the Kaweah are busily cutting deep canyons even today. There is also evidence of several periods of glacial advance in the southern Sierra. Striations (scratches) and polish on exposed rock surfaces at high elevations were created in the latest glacial period, from which we are still emerging, the ice having melted only 10-20,000 years ago. Bedrock from

Glacial erratic near Wet Meadows

which great chunks have been plucked out, as seen in the steplike topography of upper Cliff Creek, shows that rivers of ice once overrode parts of this land. Piles of rock called moraines left by melting glaciers at their farthest points of advance and along their sides are other evidence of glaciation, as are the U-shaped valleys and many of the waterfall-draped cliffs we see today.

Where glaciers widened canyons, ridges were narrowed, and the sharp comb of the Great Western Divide and of ridges like the one between Rattlesnake and Soda canyons, owe their form to erosion by ice. Most of the amphitheaterlike valleys at the heads of canyons above Mineral King and along the Great Western Divide owe their existence to the headwall plucking of glaciers.

Another readily evident factor influencing the geology of this country is the structure of the rock itself. Where the underlying granite cooled from its molten state into closely jointed masses, water has been able to penetrate and freeze. In this process — called frost wedging — the rock is broken into smaller and smaller particles until granite sand, or *grus*, like that at Sawtooth Pass or Sand Meadow, eventually is produced.

Massive granite with very little jointing tends to weather or erode in large sheets, or shells. This process is called *exfoliation*, several fine examples of which can be seen above the South Fork of the Kaweah River. The original granite of these formations has wide-spaced, nearly vertical joints. Frost wedging of the jointed mass, together with differential shrinkage of outer as compared with inner parts of the solidifying magma and the reduction

Frost wedging in granite

of pressure from above by the removal of the overlying
burden of rock by erosion, have helped produce the clean,
sheer cliffs towering over the surrounding landscape today.

Each winter and spring, avalanches bring down many
tons of debris that has been loosened from the bedrock by
frost-wedging and exfoliation. Avalanche chutes above
Cliff Creek and around Mineral King valley, among other
places, show the effects of this erosional force.

Finally, in scattered parts of this quadrangle, marble —

which is limestone changed by heat and pressure – has been weathered by the dissolving action of water containing carbon dioxide. This process has led to the formation of many beautiful caves at lower elevations of Sequoia National Park and also above Mineral King.

Thus, sedimentation in ancient seas and the intrusion of molten magma that later cooled and was uplifted by powerful forces within the earth have combined with equally impressive forces of erosion to give us the awesome and inspiring topography of this land. It is a geologic legacy matched in few other places on earth.

The Fauna

Except for the ubiquitous mosquito, birds are the most conspicuous animals that hikers encounter in the mountains. With their songs and their color, they lend a touch of delicate beauty to the Sierra scene that few other creatures can.

Several hundred species of birds occur in the area covered by this trail guide. Some of the more evident ones have been described in earlier volumes in this series. Here we would like to acquaint the reader with five High Sierra birds that a hiker is likely to see if he or she knows what to look for.

Chickadees are found wherever there are trees in the Sierra. In the high-elevation forest of Sequoia National Park, the most likely member of the genus *Parus* that hikers will see is the mountain chickadee (*Parus gambeli*). These extremely friendly little birds (less than 6" in total length) travel in small flocks through the trees, except during breeding season, when they pair off. Their constant call notes give them away — *sick-a-zee-zee* — and they are usually heard before they are seen.

Mountain chickadees are not especially colorful; they are mostly gray and white, with a black cap and a black throat. They also have a distinctive white line above the eye. They are easily told from their close relatives, the chestnut-backed chickadees found at lower elevations, by the lack of brown coloring on their backs and sides. Mountain chickadees eat low on the ecological food chain, feeding on

Blue grouse (female)

insects that they pick off leaves and twigs or find in crevices in tree bark. In turn, they are preyed on by larger birds in the Sierra food web, such as Cooper's hawk.

Another small bird that is very common in the Sierra, especially during migration, is the yellow-rumped warbler *(Dendroica coronata)*. This small, blue-gray-to-brownish bird darts through the air after flying insects, and sports a distinctive yellow rump and throat.

Whereas mountain chickadees spend the whole year in the High Sierra, yellow-rumped warblers migrate south,

Yellow-bellied marmot

or at least to lower elevations, in the winter. Also, many of them pass through *Mineral King* quadrangle while migrating between breeding grounds in Canada and wintering areas as far south as Guatemala. Their note is a loud *tchip*, and they can be seen at any elevation, from far above timberline to sequoia forests and below. During cold weather they become omnivorous, feeding on berries as well as insects.

While climbing in talus high above tree line, hikers may hear a remarkable series of chants resembling the song of the mockingbird. It comes from a far smaller bird, the rock wren (*Salpinctes obsoletus*). Wrens are usually difficult to see because their brownish coloration blends in so well with their surroundings. However, since rock wrens tend to break into song from the tops of rocks in alpine fell-fields, they are often highly visible.

They are about six inches long and grayish, with buffy patches on the tail corners (binoculars needed). However, a rolling series of notes from a small, brownish-gray bird in open rocks is generally enough to identify this summer resident of the high country. In winter these small predators migrate south into Middle America, and then return in spring when their arthropod food is again abundant.

White-throated swifts (*Aeronautes saxatalis*) also frequent the more open country of *Mineral King* quadrangle. They are black and white swallow-like birds, rather cigar-shaped, with long, pointed wings that appear to beat alternately in flight, though they actually beat in unison. White-throated swifts nest on rocky cliffs above which they fly all day long. They constantly give forth with a jeering, descending trill, *jejejejejeje*, that sounds as if they were saying, "Look at us up here so proud and free, you earthbound humans!"

White-throated swifts are insectivores, feeding on flying insects, and probably have few natural enemies because of their swift, zigzag flight. After breeding throughout the mountain regions of the West, they winter from the Southwestern U.S. down into Middle America.

Quite different from the other avian fauna briefly described here is the raven *(Corvus corax)*, a large (to 27") omnivore of the family that also includes jays, crows and magpies.

Ravens are unmistakable: all black, they often soar hawklike, alternately flapping and gliding thousands of feet in the sky over the ridges and peaks of the Great Western

Divide. The flat wings outstretched in flight, the long wedge-shaped tail and the croaking *cr-r-ruck* or *tok* calls distinguish the raven from all other large soaring birds in the Sierra.

These birds are rarely preyed upon by other animals, and they may be considered one of the top carnivores in High Sierra food chains, even though they feed chiefly on carrion. Ravens are resident in the Sierra Nevada throughout the year.

Lastly, a word of caution is in order about a non-bird found in this quadrangle. Black bears (*Ursus americanus*)

Black bear looking for easy food

are becoming increasingly bold here, and all back-country travelers, as well as car-campers, are <u>required by law</u> to secure food against bears. This means consistently using bear-proof food-storage boxes where provided, or otherwise applying the counterbalance method of suspending food in sacks over a tree limb inaccessible to bears. When a bear becomes a "problem bear," habituated to humans, it often ends up being killed. Please don't ruin your trip, and their lives, by lax and improper food storage.

This book is not a natural-history guide, and we have not attempted to tell all about the fauna to be found here. Several good books are cited in the bibliography, and readers interested in more information should refer to them.

The Flora

This chapter emphasizes that part of the flora we call trees. Not only are trees the most evident members of the plant kingdom in *Mineral King*, but they exert the greatest biotic influence on environmental conditions that determine which other plants and which animals are to be found. Trees affect the incoming solar energy and the outgoing reflected and reradiated energy, and hence they affect the temperature. They modify atmospheric humidity. They modify the wind. They change the very earth itself by their root actions, and by their litter of dead leaves, limbs and trunks which eventually return to the soil.

The most striking and impressive tree in this quadrangle, in the whole Sierra and perhaps, indeed, the world is the giant sequoia (*Sequoiadendron giganteum*). Also known as the big tree and the Sierra redwood, this is the most massive of living things, exceeding in size (though not in height) even the redwoods of coastal California. The General Sherman tree, found in the Giant Forest, is, at 275 feet high and 36.5 feet in diameter at the base, earth's largest known living thing. The estimated age of some big trees exceeds 3000 years, making them not only big but also extremely old.

Distinct in wood structure, needle shape, cone size, physiology and growth form from the coast redwood, big trees are also distinct in their range. They are found naturally only on the west slope of the Sierra from about 4700 to 7500 feet in elevation in scattered groves from

Kelley's lily

Placer County south to Tulare County. The origin of these
groves and the discontinuous distribution of the species,
which once occurred widely in the Northern Hemisphere,
are poorly understood. However, ancient forest fires,
landslides and avalanches, as well as the apparent
westward migration of the sequoia along ridge lines as the
Sierra uplifted and glaciers advanced, most certainly had
some bearing on the present location of these stately plants.

Ecologists now realize that periodic forest fires and
other disturbance factors are <u>required</u> by this tree for its
survival as a species. Even John Muir noticed that big-tree
seedlings and saplings were much more abundant in places
that evidenced past disturbances, such as logging and

landslides, than in undisturbed areas. Today it is well-recognized that the majority of regeneration under big-tree stands in the mid-elevation Sierra consists of white firs and incense-cedars rather than big trees. These two species thrive under the shade of big trees, and their seeds germinate much more readily in undisturbed forest litter than do the seeds of big trees. On the other hand, white fir and incense-cedar are extremely susceptible to destruction by fire, especially in their early years. Hence, an intensive program of fire control and an end to logging in big-tree groves over the past 80 years have actually had a detrimental effect on the overall survival of big-tree seedlings in the Sierra.

However, big trees are not on the verge of dying out due to fire control. Eighty or even 800 years without regeneration can't be too damaging to a plant species whose individuals live to a reproductive age of more than 3000 years. Perhaps the greatest enemy of the big tree is human technology. Road-building, the millions of human feet brought in on the roads, the trampling by these feet on the shallow soil over fragile roots in the more popular groves, and perhaps that ubiquitous symbol of our great civilization, smog, will do them in sooner than all the fire "protection" we give the trees. Already, ponderosa pine is being exterminated in the San Bernardino Mountains of Southern California by photochemical smog blown in from the Los Angeles Basin. Smog damage has been found in trees near San Diego, in the San Francisco Bay Area and above Fresno. Ecologist E.F. Watt of the University of California at Davis has predicted that trees will be a thing of the past in California after the year 2000. We hope he is wrong: if the trees go, what of us?

Hikers on trails described in this guidebook will see big trees at Atwell Mill, along the South Fork of the Kaweah and in Mountain Home State Forest.

The tree most often found as an understory species in big-tree stands, as well as in some other types of forest, is white fir *(Abies concolor)*. In contrast to other cone-bearing trees, the true firs have upright cones that disintegrate on the tree, rather than persistent cones that hang down. Their needles are also distinctive, being flat in cross section and occurring singly rather than in bunches, as in the pines.

The long process of change in plant and animal life from a simple, harsh community, such as lichen on a rock, to a more complex and hospitable community of life, such as a meadow or forest, is called *succession*. White fir occurs late in succession, as evidenced by its position as an understory tree in big-tree and other forests. Because it is able to regenerate in the shade of other, earlier successional plants, it is considered a "shade-tolerant" species.

However, white fir is not tolerant of fire. From early to middle age, it is a thin-barked tree easily killed by even relatively "cool" forest fires. Where fires have occurred frequently in the past, the earlier-in-succession (fire-resistant) pines and big trees are much more common than white fir. So by observing the kinds of trees in a forest, hikers can gain some insight into its history and where it might be going.

Users of this guide will find white fir common below 8000 feet in most of the area covered by the book. The red-barked fir trees with cones of 9" (versus white fir's 5" maximum) found at higher elevations are either red fir or Shasta red fir (*Abies magnifica*).

Not very impressive when seen with big trees, but a forest giant among other trees in the Sierra, is the sugar pine (*Pinus lambertiana*). It attains a height of over 225 feet and a diameter of nearly ten feet. This tree's cones are perhaps even more impressive than the rest of the plant, for they occasionally attain lengths of over 24", easily the longest cones of any American conifer, and are sought after for decorative purposes. Another identifying characteristic of sugar pine is its needles, which occur in bundles of five. The distinctive bark of large, mature trees consists of vertical ridges of loose purplish scales. Sugar pine ranges from Oregon to Baja California. In *Mineral King*, hikers are most likely to find it along the Garfield/Hockett and Summit Meadow trails.

Another 5-needle pine, which users of the higher trails above 10,000 feet will see, is foxtail pine (*Pinus balfouriana*). This plant is drought-resistant and is found on open, rocky slopes, often with a dry southwest exposure.

Foxtail pine is so named because of the bushy habit of its foliage, which is retained for many years on the branch. The tree's cones are short (to 4") and pendant. Because of the exposed and harsh conditions under which this tree usually exists, it is often gnarled and bent, and rarely attains a height of greater than 40 feet. Hikers who have been to the Ancient Bristlecone Pine Forest in the White Mountains of eastern California will notice the close similarity between foxtail and its close relative, bristlecone pine (not found in the Sierra).

Many other trees, shrubs and wildflowers are mentioned in this trail guide. It is impossible to cite much less describe them all here, so the reader's attention is called to several natural-history books listed in the bibliography for a more extensive treatment of the Sierra flora.

Foxtail pines above Ansel Lake

The Climate

California's weather and hence that of the Sierra Nevada is governed by what goes on 2000 miles away, out over the Pacific Ocean. There, a permanent system of high pressure called the Pacific High moves north and south with the yearly march of the sun. In summer it is nearly due west of central California; in winter it lies off Baja California, Mexico.

When the Pacific High sits between the California coast and the subpolar low-pressure area in the Gulf of Alaska during summer, it tends to keep the North Pacific's storms, bred in this low, from reaching the state. However, during the winter, the Pacific High is farther south, and also not as strong, while the subpolar low has increased in intensity. That's when storms move off the ocean over the land, and California gets rained on — or snowed on. Actually, it's not all that simple, but this brief sketch does help explain why about 95% of the precipitation in *Mineral King* occurs from November through March, while only 5% or so comes during the summer, when most readers of this guide are likely to visit the mountains.

What about that 5%? It takes the form of short, afternoon thunderstorms. When hot air from the Central Valley, or more rarely the Owens Valley, rises up the slopes of the Sierra, it cools at a rate of about 5.5 degrees F per 1000 feet of altitude gain. In addition, the air over heat-radiating surfaces in the high country, such as an expanse of whitish granite, may rise convectionally. When air rises, for whatever reason, it cools, and may be forced to drop its moisture. A thundershower is born. It "never rains in the Sierra in summer" — but a poncho or lightweight tent is not that heavy, and wet sleeping bags just don't work. In fact, intense storms can occur in any month.

Summer temperatures in the mountains vary with elevation and slope *aspect* — compass orientation. Generally, the temperature in stable air decreases by about 3.6 degrees F for every 1000-foot gain in elevation. So, disregarding aspect, a difference in air temperature of about 30 degrees F can be expected between Clough Cave Ranger Station (3600') — the lowest trailhead in the book — and Franklin Pass (11760') — the highest trail described — due to change in elevation alone. The average hiker is not likely to make this trip in one day, but the possibilities are dramatic. When we add to this the chilling effect of wind, a windless 80-degree afternoon at Clough Cave turns into a skin-felt experience of 30 degrees at Franklin Pass, assuming a 25-mile-per-hour wind there. A windbreaker is another vital piece of summer paraphernalia.

One last comment on climate: solar radiation reaching the earth's surface increases with elevation. There is about twice as much ultraviolet energy at 14,000 feet as at sea level, and ultraviolet causes sunburn. So visitors to the high country who burn easily, who haven't acquired a good tan by the time they start living out in the sun, or who simply want to avoid getting skin cancer someday, do well to liberally apply a reliable ultraviolet sunscreen while here.

Travel

Since this is a hiking guide and neither motor vehicles nor bicycles are permitted on trails in Sequoia National Park or Golden Trout Wilderness, a brief statement on how to get around on foot in Mineral King is in order here. We usually refer to this method as backpacking.

There are as many reasons for backpacking as there are backpackers. One of the most frequently cited reasons has something to do with "getting away from it all," and this usually means going where there aren't very many other people.

It has been claimed that the density of humanity in the mountains varies inversely with the *square of the distance* from a road, and with the *cube of the elevation* above the road. To this might be added a third exponent: the density of humanity also varies inversely with the *fourth power of a route's "off-trail-ness,"* meaning the degree to which it is poorly marked or cross country. The hiker planing a trip in Sequoia National Park can, by combining the trail descriptions and mileages with the topographic map in this volume, obtain a pretty fair idea of the probability of finding seclusion here.

In the Sierra, where roads ends, trails begin; and there are two marvelous inventions designed to take us along any trail in *Mineral King* quadrangle. They are standard equipment for most everyone, and they stay with the hiker every step of the way. These tough, tender, smelly or sweet appendages way down at the other end are called feet.

Coupled with a good back, and the right boots and pack, they are all one really needs to do anything in this book.

The best footwear for backpackers' feet in the Sierra Nevada are ankletop leather boots with Vibram soles. They should be moderately heavy but flexible, and *well broken-in*. Waterproofing is an invaluable treatment and should be done *regularly*, using a wax such as *Sno-Seal*, rather than an oil, which softens the leather and thus reduces support of the feet. Becoming more popular and in common use on trails are combination synthetic/leather, and even totally synthetic, hiking boots. We are still partial to all-leather boots due to their superior durability and support characteristics, though they are getting increasingly hard to find and costly, compared to the synthetics.

The best backpack for trail walking in the Sierra has two parts: a frame and a pack. Usually the frame is welded tubular aluminum and the pack is coated nylon. Backpacks with padded waist belts save the hips, and padded shoulder straps save the shoulders. The nylon-mesh back rest is superior to the solid nylon bands because of its broader distribution of weight and its greater breathability. Internal-frame backpacks, as opposed to the traditional external-frame type, are being used extensively in the backcountry today. They hug the body more and give better balance, but have poor ventilation and lead to sweatier backs, and generally allow less volume to be carried.

When two feet and a back plus boots and backpack start up a trail in this quadrangle, it is called backpacking, the most popular, economical and ecologically sound method of travel in the mountains today.

And just to help insure that there are clean, unspoiled mountains to backpack in, now and in the future, we'd like to summarize a few of the many ways that each of us can help ensure the preservation of *Mineral King* and other mountain mansions.

First of all, be sure to obtain your wilderness permit and to adhere to the limitations meant to lessen our collective impact on fragile alpine places. Many mountain sites are being trampled to death by increasing numbers of travelers. Park Service and Forest Service quotas on the numbers allowed each day into impacted areas are meant to help slow this environmental damage.

Go light. John Muir went into the hills with little more than a pocketful of biscuits and his overcoat and sketch pad.

Don't camp in meadows. Use "hard" campsites, such as sandy and rocky areas, that can take more use.

Standing timber, alive or dead, should never be cut in the backcountry except in the direst emergency. Use gas stoves for cooking and build small campfires or none at all (they are now *prohibited* in many areas). Check with rangers for current regulations in effect, particularly late in the season when fire danger tends to be highest.

Use only well-established campsites and don't create new fire rings. Officially, camping is permitted only 100 feet or farther from lakes and streams in Sierra wilderness areas now, and *nothing* should go into any body of water in the mountains. And this means toothpaste, spaghetti pasta and *any kind* of soap, no matter how "biodegradable." *Anything* put into mountain streams is pollution, and some of our once-pristine bodies of water are already unfit to drink due to thoughtless campers. Wash yourself and your dishes in a basin or dish and dispose of your washwater far from lake or stream in sandy soil.

All unburnable garbage should be packed out of the backcountry. This includes aluminum foil, *which is not burnable,* and is the most pervasive and indestructible form of trash polluting the mountains today. If you should find some in a fireplace left by another party, don't be embarrassed to pack it out.

Bury all human waste several inches deep in organic soils whenever possible, and burn your toilet paper when it is safe to do so. Do this 100 feet or more from water, trails, and campsites.

Use switchbacks. They were built to save the slopes, and shortcutting them causes erosion and destroys the slopes.

Both backpackers and car campers should note that in the past few years, an increase in raids by black bears on improperly stored food has led to a great deal of damage to equipment (including cars) and to the unwelcome curtailing of many trips due to losses of food in the backcountry. Be sure to store all food safely (and legally) whenever away from your camp, whether in the backcountry or in a campground. Check with rangers for the latest recommendations. When bears become too habituated to humans, they always lose. So help save your trip and the bears' lives. Many backcountry as well as frontcountry campsites in Sequoia National Park now have bearproof food-storage boxes (see trail descriptions). Food storage cannisters for backpackers are available at

Mineral King Ranger Station. They weigh less than 3 pounds, are completely bearproof and will hold enough food for several days. Contact the station for more information. There is even a bearproof food storage *building* in Mineral King near the ranger station, so no food need be left in vehicles while hikers are on the trail. Please make use of these aids to (in the end) bear preservation.

Ultimately mountain travellers should strive for minimum impact: taking only pictures and leaving only footprints. For once the wilderness is gone, it will never come back.

We recommend the Wilderness Press publication *Backpacking Basics* for more detailed coverage of enlightened travel in the mountains.

Bear box at Cliff Creek campsite

The Trails

Most of the trails described in this book are not generally considered to be easy trails. Most of them, particularly those beginning at Mineral King itself, start out steep and dusty. But the feeling of accomplishment that sweeps over the hiker as he or she tops a high alpine pass in this region can be known only to those who get there on their own two legs. These trails are for the fit afoot.

In this guide we describe eight main trails and seven secondary trails in the *Mineral King* quadrangle. Connecting trails to the north are described in the High Sierra Hiking Guide to *Triple Divide Peak*, and to the south, in *Exploring the Southern Sierra*, vol. 2.

MAIN TRAILS

The main trails described in this book are overnight backpacking trails, demanding thorough preparation and familiarity with outdoor manners—see the chapter "Travel". Starting from roadends in Sequoia National Park and Mountain Home State Forest, they are the mountain traveler's main access to the high country. Some of the shorter routes described here, and the beginning parts of the longer ones, could be done as day walks by hikers in good condition. Due to the steepness of the trails, however, we have decided not to designate any of them as strictly day hikes, since many walkers would find them too strenuous for one-day excursions.

The secondary trails described here generally are short connections between main trails or little-used alternative routes to less-visited areas. They usually afford more seclusion and naturalness than the main trails do, and they may require some route-finding ability.

Please note that all map references in this and the next section of the book are to the 1986 Wilderness Press edition of the *Mineral King* quadrangle map.

THE TRAILHEADS

The Mineral King section of Sequoia National Park is at the end of 25-mile-long Mineral King road, which is steep, winding and partly unpaved. The road leaves State Route 198 about three miles northeast of Three Rivers and gains 6700 feet in its climb up the canyon of the East Fork of the Kaweah River. The drive takes over an hour. If you are planning to camp in a campground before or during your hiking in the Mineral King area, be sure to check the sign at Highway 198 on the availability of campsites up the road. This will avoid great disappointment and having to drive back down the road a considerable distance to find legal camping.

There are presently four parking areas in Mineral King Valley. Unfortunately, there have been numerous incidents of marmot attacks on brake lines and other rubber hoses on automobiles parked here. Please check with the rangers about what precautions to take to prevent this type of damage to your car. The first parking area is north of the road about 1 mile east of the Ranger Station (map section C1). No trails originate from this parking lot.

The second lot, the trailhead for Timber Gap, Monarch Lakes, and Sawtooth Pass, lies astride the road just before "Harry's Bend," in map section D1, about a mile from the ranger station. This lot tends to be crowded with vehicles all summer.

Parking for patrons of the Mineral King Pack Station (only) provided at the pack station ¼ mile beyond the bend, just past the turnoff to the permittee cabins (map section D2). The road beyond the pack station toward Farewell Gap is closed to vehicles.

Hikers bound for the lakes south of Mineral King, for Farewell Gap or for Franklin Pass may park in the lot in the permittee cabins area (map section D2). Turn right before the pack station, cross the East Fork Kaweah River on a bridge, and park at the end of the road near the phone booth.

The Paradise Peak and Atwell/Hockett trails start at Atwell Mill Campground, about four miles west of Mineral King on the Mineral King road (map section B1). Park at the *east* end of the campground.

The Garfield/Hockett and South Fork trails start at the Clough Cave Ranger Station and Campground about 13 miles from Highway 198 on South Fork Drive (just west of map section A4, in the *Kaweah* quadrangle).

From the south, hikers heading to Summit and Maggie Lakes start at Shake Camp in Mountain Home State

East Fork Kaweah River

Forest (just south of map section B5, in the *Camp Nelson* quadrangle). This trailhead is reached from Porterville via State Route 190, county roads J37/M239 (which begins 1 mile beyond Springville) and M220 to Mountain Home State Forest. Then follow M247 past the pack station to the trailhead, which is at the entrance to Shake Camp Campground (total distance from Highway 190: about 23 miles).

WILDERNESS PERMITS

After March 1, trail permits for Sequoia National Park may be obtained in advance by writing or FAXing Sequoia National Park Wilderness Office, Three Rivers, CA 93271 — (209) 565-3797. Requests must be made at least 21 days before your hike, and approximately ⅔ of the permits are available in advance. The remaining ⅓ of the permits will be available on a walk-in basis the afternoon before your hike at the visitor center or ranger station nearest the trailhead. There are no trailhead quotas for the Golden Trout Wilderness, Sequoia National Forest. Forest Service permits are available at Sequoia National Forest Headquarters, 900 West Grand, Porterville, CA 93257, and at the Tule River Ranger Station, 32588 Highway 190, Springville, CA 93265.

Hikers going from National Park to National Forest land, or vice versa, may use the same permit in both areas, and may obtain it from either agency, provided the proper codes have been entered on the permits.

NO WOOD FIRES ALLOWED ABOVE 9000 FEET IN THE KAWEAH RIVER DRAINAGE (and no fires at all in the Mineral King Valley drainage).

Trail Descriptions

The trail descriptions that follow often mention *ducks* and *blazes*. A duck is one or several small rocks placed upon a larger rock in such a way that the placement is obviously not natural. A blaze is a scar on a tree trunk, often in the form of the letter " i " at about eye level to mark the route of a trail.

It should be noted also that neither dogs nor firearms are allowed on National *Park* trails described in this guide. Bicycles are not allowed on *any* National *Park* trails nor in National *Forest* Wilderness areas. All map references, again, are to the 1986 edition of the *Mineral King* quadrangle published by Wilderness Press, *not* to the map published by the US Geological Survey.

Campers should be aware too of increasing contamination of surface waters by an intestinal protozoan known as *Giardia lamblia*, which can be carried and spread by both wild and domestic animals, as well as by humans. It is now recommended that *all* stream and lake water be either boiled, chemically treated or filtered before drinking. Most large outdoor equipment suppliers have effective products for sale, though simple boiling remains the surest method of purifying water containing *Giardia* or other pathogens.

Special campfire and other regulations are in effect in several areas of the *Mineral King* quadrangle to help preserve the environment. Also, proper food storage, secure from bears, is *now required by law* and is *enforced*, in Sequoia National Park. So hikers should be sure to learn about and observe these regulations in order that there will be a Mineral King tomorrow too.

MAIN TRAIL #1

Mineral King to Little Claire Lake
via Sawtooth Pass (18 miles)

This route to Little Claire Lake climbs over the Great Western Divide beyond Sawtooth Pass, descends Lost Canyon, and crosses to Soda Creek before rising steeply to the lake. The segment of this trail between Monarch Lakes and Sawtooth Pass is in such bad repair, and is so difficult to find and to negotiate, that we no longer recommend doing this hike in this direction. However, so many hikers consider this *the* classic gateway to the backcountry from Mineral King that here we still describe the route, as we have in previous editions of this guidebook. Hikers are now advised, though, to start out on either the Franklin Pass Trail or the Timber Gap Trail (Main Trails #2 and #6) and to do a loop, *returning* to Mineral King via Sawtooth Pass if desired. Walking is steep from the start, but the views from these passes are extraordinary, and once east of the divide, one is not likely to encounter many other people.

We start in the parking area (map section D1) one mile above Mineral King Ranger Station and immediately begin climbing in open chaparral toward Sawtooth Pass, 6 miles ahead.

After 1 mile of steep climbing we come to a fork and go right. Timber Gap lies 2 miles to the left (Main Trail #6). Our route climbs through Sierra juniper on shaly rock toward Monarch Creek, which soon appears in cascades far below the trail. From here to Groundhog Meadow (not labeled on the topo), the trail climbs above the stream, and along the way we have views-to-be-contemplated up and down the glacially carved canyon.

At Groundhog Meadow we take the right fork across Monarch Creek. The left fork is an abandoned trail with forks to Sawtooth and Glacier passes, and the Park Service requests that it *not* be used due to erosion problems. We immediately pass a fair campsite and begin a series of long switchbacks which take us through open stands of red fir, silver pine and foxtail pine with an understory of chinquapin, currant, gooseberry and lupine. After many switchbacks the trail crosses a ridge in timber, and just beyond the next bend is a nice lunch stop, where there is water 100 yards out on the hillside. Shortly beyond we come to a signed junction with the trail to Crystal Lake.

(The 1½-mile lateral to Crystal Lake climbs across open slopes dotted with lodgepole and foxtail pine, zigzagging steeply up to a notch (10400') from which we can see below the two small Cobalt Lakes. Then we descend into the Crystal Creek drainage and pass a faint trail leading to Cobalt Lakes, where camping is especially scenic. The lower lake has a small self-sustaining population of brook trout. Continuing past this trail, we climb over metavolcanic rocks past foxtail pines to a narrow bench. At the

south end of this bench is the Crystal Lake dam (10788')
built in 1911 and still operational. The lake lies in a glacial
cirque with a beautiful granitic/metamorphic contact running through it. South and east of the lake, the rocks are
granitic; on the north and west sides they are metamorphic.
The lake has a self-sustaining population of brook trout.
The only decent campsites are on the bench below the dam,
but the sunsets here are unrivaled.)

Back on the main trail to Monarch Lakes, we round a
shoulder and can see Timber Gap to the north and the
Great Western Divide and Sawtooth Pass up ahead. We
cross two forks of Monarch Creek and arrive at Lower
Monarch Lake (10380'), where camping is good but wood
fires are not allowed. Campers are required to use the toilet
facilities and the bear-proof food-storage boxes now in
place at the lake. A well-defined path goes around the
north side of the lake and climbs through willows to Upper
Monarch Lake (10640'), which is dammed and lacks
campsites.

The trail to Sawtooth Pass continues north and drops
a little through willows and corn lilies to a junction. Here
we turn right and begin climbing steeply past paintbrush,
wild buckwheat and various yellow composites — flowers
related to daisies — north up the ridge. One is well-advised
to stay to the left and not to get onto the steep, loose, granite
sand that leads directly up toward the pass, despite
footprints there. Instead, we follow ducks toward the ridge
to the north. From this ridge we traverse east toward the
main crest. There are numerous "bootleg" trails going every
which way up here and the actual trail is ill-defined.

Do your best to get to the main ridge and then follow ducks on a route that stays close to the crest all the way to Sawtooth Pass (11600'), which is higher than the lowest point on the crest. Photographers who are here at sunset will find the lighting and alpenglow on the Sierra crest to the east an optical delight. The Central Valley smog in the west rarely fails to produce a brilliant orange sunset.

From the ridge our ducked route drops steeply and deviously on granite down the east side of the pass to Columbine Lake (10900'), where camping is best in late season at the western end. The scenery is spectacular, with the fractured granites of Sawtooth Peak looming over the lake to the south. In midseason here shooting stars cover the meadows with pink brilliance. Be aware that smart,

Columbine Lake

hungry bears can be a problem here, as there arc no convenient places to store food safely.

We circle the lake on its north side and cross the outlet, which may be tricky in high water, and then climb over a low saddle (actually part of the Great Western Divide) into the drainage of the Kern River. The trail drops on steep, short switchbacks into Lost Canyon as we look ahead to forested Chagoopa Plateau and the deeply incised trench of the Kern River.

Numerous sites for camping present themselves along Lost Canyon Creek, although it is about a mile before we get into timber, where secondary succession of the vegetation is occurring after extensive avalanches a decade ago. The casual bird-watcher here will likely notice the natty white-crowned sparrow, the drab green-tailed towhee, the raucous Clark's nutcracker and the delicate-blue mountain bluebird.

After crossing the stream to the south side, our trail leaves the *Mineral King* quadrangle and enters the *Kern Peak* quadrangle. Continuing in *Kern Peak*, we recross to the north side of the creek and reach a signed junction with a trail to Big 5 Lakes. (This trail climbs in a series of switchbacks through lodgepole pine and silver pine up to a bench, which it crosses near a small, shallow lake. It then drops steeply, as it re-enters the *Mineral King* quadrangle, to the outlet of Big 5 Lake #1, where an outlet crossing is made on logs. The well-defined route goes past several good campsites on the lake's north side before climbing to a junction with the trail connecting Big 5 and Little 5 lakes — see Main Trail #6).

Our route down Lost Canyon continues to a third crossing back to the south side of the stream, where we go through an area recovering from fire. We then round the ridge that separates Lost Canyon and Soda Creek, and descend through chinquapin and manzanita to a trail junction just above Soda Creek. The trail to the left goes down to Big Arroyo; to the right is the Soda Creek trail. Our route is the latter, and we turn upstream toward Little Claire Lake, 5 miles away.

The trail climbs gently through a mixed forest of red fir and silver, lodgepole and Jeffrey pine. The observant hiker will note evidence of avalanches along here, and

Looking up Lost Canyon to Sawtooth Peak

perhaps will see that they tend to perpetuate an open forest or a scrub growth, which in the nomenclature of ecologists is a *subclimax*. Avalanches interrupt the development of climax vegetation, probably fir forest at this elevation. We eventually come to a crossing of Soda Creek, after re-entering *Mineral King* quadrangle, and our route becomes suddenly steeper. The path climbs on switchbacks through mixed forest and then under foxtail pines, leveling out just before Little Claire Lake (10400'). Here, due to a fragile subalpine environment and heavy usage, campsites must be made 100 feet or more from the lakeshore, and fires are essentially prohibited due to lack of wood. The pine marten, a member of the weasel family, lives around here, and one may be lucky – and quiet – enough to see one.

(The route from Mineral King to Little Claire Lake via Franklin Pass is described as Main Trail #2.)

MAIN TRIAL #2

Mineral King to Little Claire Lake
via Franklin Pass (12 miles)

The Franklin Pass Trail described here takes us past Franklin Lakes, over Franklin Pass on the Great Western Divide, and down into Rattlesnake Canyon before climbing to Forester and Little Claire lakes. The switchbacks above Franklin Lakes have been re-engineered, making this route to the lakes beyond the Great Western Divide considerably easier than the Sawtooth Pass Trail (Main Trail #1).

Hikers taking the Franklin Pass/Farewell Gap Trail must park at the Eagle Crest trailhead; you should not park at the pack station.

At the start (map section D2), we walk by the Mineral King Pack Station and proceed up a dirt road through open scrub-sagebrush, gooseberry, currant and willow — with the East Fork Kaweah River gurgling on our right. Farewell Gap and Vandever Mountain are visible straight ahead. We ford Crystal Creek and at a signed fork veer left onto the Franklin Pass/Farewell Gap Trail.

Our route climbs east through some young black cottonwoods — note their distinctive and pungent odor — and then fords Franklin Creek. Here we begin a long series of switchbacks up Farewell Canyon, where only occasional patches of red fir give shade on a hot sunny afternoon. The valley below us is V-shaped in cross section possibly because after the glacier melted from its **U**-shaped canyon, the stream cut deep into the relatively soft metamorphic and sedimentary substrata. On this stretch of trail the results of switchback-cutting are particularly unsightly, and hikers who want to preserve the scenery and prevent erosion will stay on the trail.

At about 9300' the trail forks. The right branch goes on to Farewell Gap and Hockett Meadows (Main Trail #3), but we continue ahead toward Franklin Pass. Our route climbs through stands of juniper and foxtail pine into silver pine and red fir, where red paintbrush, purplish phlox, blue gentian and creamy corn lily give color to the ground cover as we approach our second crossing of Franklin Creek. There are some poor campsites near the crossing.

Along the trail here, entomologists may recognize Acmon blue butterflies, which are small and blue with an orangish trailing edge on the wing. They are commonly seen at wet spots along the route.

Long switchbacks in metamorphosed rocks carry us past fair campsites on Franklin Creek below the dam on Lower Franklin Lake (10300'). On the lake itself, there are only a few fair sites, on the north slope. Camping in the exposed sites on the north slope must be done 100 feet or more from the water's edge. Campers are urged to make use of the pit toilet and food-storage boxes at the lower lake. However, hikers with the inclination and the time can continue climbing on the trail above the lower lake in foxtail-pine forest to several beautiful if treeless campsites situated on a bench above the lake. Upper Franklin Lake (10600') is a short hike across boulders from here, and the sunsets are unparalleled. Both these lakes support good populations of eastern brook trout.

From the campsites above Lower Franklin Lake, the trail ascends steadily by switchbacks nearly 1200' to Franklin Pass (11760'). Hikers are urged to hike on the trail on both sides of the pass and not to cut switchbacks, in order to prevent erosion and reduce trail-maintenance costs. Lifting our gaze to the surrounding panorama, we are rewarded with alpine scenery, from the Kaweah Peaks on the north to the Whitney group in the east. Ahead is the drainage of the Kern River, while back to the west is the Kaweah watershed we have left. We are on the Great Western Divide.

The trail makes a long swing to the north in granite

Historical note: the west boundary of Sequoia Park is now far west of here

sand and we overlook a series of unnamed lakes below
Rainbow Mountain before switchbacking down into
Rattlesnake Canyon. After passing through stands of
lodgepole interspersed with meadows, we come to a junction with the trail to Shotgun Pass (Secondary Trail #3). A
quarter mile below this junction, the trail forks. The right
fork crosses Rattlesnake Creek, recrosses after ¼ mile,
and veers north away from the stream before rejoining it
for a long drop to the Kern River. The left fork, which is
our route, takes us one mile to Forester Lake, which is
surrounded by good campsites. (An unmapped trail leads
right (south) to Rattlesnake Creek.)

We continue north and west from Forester Lake along a ducked trail, cross a cascading stream lined with shooting stars, heather, and Labrador tea, and climb to a small meadow on a bench. Mountain bluebirds and chickadees may be seen here, as we resume climbing in an open forest of foxtail pines. The white granite soil and the well-spaced, weathered and gnarled trees resemble the Ancient Bristlecone Pine Forest of the White Mountains in eastern California, where environmental conditions are similar.

At the top of this climb we cross a low pass and quickly wind down to Little Claire Lake, where camping is excellent. Due to heavy use, camping is not allowed within 100

Little Claire Lake

feet of the lakeshore, and fires are essentially prohibited. (A loop trip can be made by returning to Mineral King over Sawtooth Pass or Timber Gap — see Main Trail #1 or #6.)

MAIN TRAIL #3

Mineral King/Hockett Meadows Loop
(35 miles)

For a pleasant, early-season, week-long trip in mostly forested country at relatively low elevations, the Hockett Meadows loop trail is ideal, though mosquitoey. Snow melts earlier here than in the high country, and the trails have rather gentle gradients. This trip takes us over Farewell Gap into the drainage of the Little Kern River. Farther on, anglers should have success along the South Fork of the Kaweah. The return from Hockett Meadows to Mineral King is across forested north-facing slopes high above the East Fork Kaweah River. (This trail may also be walked in reverse, giving one a gentler first-day climb through Tar Gap.)

At first, our route is the Franklin Pass Trail (Main Trail #2), which we take to the junction 2 miles below Farewell Gap (in map section D2) where we turn right (south). From here the trail climbs steadily across mostly open slopes where wild onion and Indian paintbrush are abundant in mid-season. We cross many streamlets that flow until late in the year, and in some years there is a patch of late-melting snow below the gap until mid season. When the lighting is right, it is easy to make out numerous game trails on the slope below Vandever Mountain to the west.

At Farewell Gap (10587') we leave Sequoia National Park and enter Golden Trout Wilderness in Sequoia National Forest. Far off to the south is the southern end of the Sierra Nevada, above the Kern River, and in the immediate foreground lie the headwaters of one of its tributaries, the Little Kern River. A sea of blue lupine flowers extends down the slope.

From Farewell Gap we switchback down over dark, exposed metamorphic rocks, which are more reminiscent of the dry desert ranges to the east than of the granitic Sierra Nevada. The trail splits at the bottom of the

Glacial erratics below Bullfrog Lakes

switchbacks and we take the lower (right) branch, heading down the canyon. (The left branch of the trail more or less contours around to a junction with the Bullfrog Lakes Trail, going off to the east. The route to the two Bullfrog Lakes is steep but short. They offer scenic, if exposed, camping in a spot where a striking contact between granitic and metamorphic rocks gives evidence of the geologic forces at work in these mountains. The only place to safely store food from bears is in trees on a bench below the lakes.)

Beyond this fork we descend in open brush toward the Little Kern. Where the trail levels out, there are campsites across the stream in a stand of foxtail pines. Then we begin to drop again through sagebrush, lupine, manzanita and bitter cherry.

At the next fork in the trail, an unmaintained short-cut contours ahead to meet the trail going toward Silver Lake, Shotgun Pass and Lion Meadows (Secondary Trails #3 and #6). We drop off to the right toward Wet Meadows.

Across the Little Kern is what remains of Broder's cabin, a line camp and part of an early-1900s pack operation. It's a fair campsite. We pass another fork (not shown on the map) from which a trail to the left switchbacks up toward the trails to Silver Lake and Shotgun Pass and to Lion Meadows (Secondary Trails #3 and #6). Then we drop steadily above the miniature gorge of the Little Kern in crunchy metamorphics to a campsite on the river, in a stand of lodgepole, fir and juniper. At the campsite we turn right at the signs where the route ahead is an unmaintained one down the river (see Secondary Trail #6). Our route crosses the stream here on logs, descends above the river, and then begins climbing to the right in mountain chaparral and soon enters dense red-fir forest, where deer tracks are often more evident than humans' or horses' in the trail dust. The outlet stream from Wet Meadows is the first water since the Little Kern. We cross it and climb, now in granite, to another trail fork. The trail to the left (south) goes toward the Little Kern River and Quinn Patrol Cabin (see Secondary Trails #6 and #7).

Here our route continues ahead toward Wet Meadows and Hockett Meadows. We come to another packer camp, Deadman Camp, beside a pasture where there are a weather station and a snow course. Data gathered here give irrigation and power companies some idea of the next season's runoff from this area.

A short climb through chaparral brings us to a level stretch shaded by lodgepole, and we pass a trail heading north through Wet Meadows (with debris-littered packer sites) that rejoins our main route in 1 mile. Then, after several more stream crossings, passing a littered, broken-down cabin and some gentle switchbacks through lodgepole forest, we arrive at the Wet Meadows Entrance of Sequoia National Park. Among the various signs here, one tells us that this is national-park land, and firearms and pets are not allowed on the trails. (The trail *ahead* soon forks, the left fork heading southwest through soggy meadows to Windy Gap, where it meets laterals to Quinn Patrol Cabin and Summit Lake (Secondary Trail #7 and Main Trail #8). The right branch ahead drops to a junction with the trail we continue on toward Blossom Lakes.)

Turning right, our route from here leads north, along

a ridge that delineates the Park/Forest boundary, toward
Blossom Lakes 2 miles away. After about a mile we come
to another fork. (The rough but well-ducked trail to the
right shortly drops off the ridge to the marshy lower lake of
the Blossom Lakes group. It is undergoing succession from
lake to forest, and the upper end has already become a
swale covered with shooting stars, willows, wild onions and
knotweed. Camping is rather unscenic and the campsite
where the trail meets the lowest Blossom Lake is often
occupied. Fishing is good here for brook trout only during
early season. The more secluded upper lakes of this chain
are reached by cross-country scrambling. Here fishing
remains good throughout the season.)

Back at the previous fork we continue on toward
Hockett Meadows, rejoining the trail that branched off at
the Wet Meadows Entrance and dropping steadily through
lodgepole forest where seed-eating juncos are common,
especially in late season. We gradually descend to a ford of
Hunter Creek and come to a trail junction. The trail to the
left (south-east) crosses Hunter Creek and climbs steadily
beside an unnamed tributary, reaching Windy Gap in about
two miles (see Main Trail #8).

Our route continues ahead in lodgepole pine forest to
South Fork Meadows, which is popular with stock parties
and anglers using the Garfield/Hockett Trail (Main Trail
#7). Fishing is good here for small-sized brook trout until
late in the season.

Beyond the Meadows the trail branches again. This
time the left branch (the Tuohy Cutoff) crosses the South
Fork of the Kaweah and swings south and west to meet the

Tuohy Trail along Tuohy Creek in about 2½ miles (see Main Trails #7 and #8). We go *right* and soon reach another junction.

Ahead the trail goes to shallow Hockett Lakes and meets the Garfield/Hockett Trail (Main Trail #7). Here we go right (north) toward Hockett Meadows. Our route skirts several meadows while climbing gently in lodgepole-pine forest to the northeast corner of Sand Meadow and another trail junction. This time it's the Hockett Lakes cutoff, which goes back left (southwest) toward Hockett Lakes and the South Fork of the Kaweah. We go right again and soon emerge from timber at the bridged crossing of Whitman Creek in Hockett Meadows. At this end is Hockett Ranger Station, and a Park Service ranger is here most of the summer to help hikers. It's nice to stop in for a chat. Limited camping (bear box available) is allowed in the forest near the meadows, which are loaded with small fish (in Whitman Creek) and wildflowers. Another campsite with food-storage cable and toilet is located nearby just off the trail to Evelyn Lake and Cahoon Rock (Secondary Trail #4), which we pass just north of the ranger station.

Our trail enters increasingly dense timber which grades from lodgepole pine into red fir, and fortunate travelers may hear the trumpetlike call of the pileated woodpecker. This crow-sized bird is a close relative of the ivory-billed woodpecker, formerly of eastern forests and now extinct in the United States. Other evidence of the pileated woodpecker is the oblong feeding holes it makes in insect-infested trees.

At Horse Creek there is a fair campsite with a food-storage cable. Just beyond this crossing we intersect the unsigned trail to Ansel Lake, where camping is much more scenic, though the route is obscure and difficult to follow. The lake is more easily approached by a short cross-country jaunt from either Eagle Lake or Upper White Chief Meadows (see Main Trails #4 and #5).

Shortly we pass the trail to Atwell Mill (Secondary Trail #1) and begin what is essentially a long contour in mixed forest above the East Fork canyon toward Mineral King. Several overlooks along the route give us good views of the smog creeping in from the Central Valley 50 miles away. In late season, the air looks especially dirty.

Numerous streams bounding in from the high open slopes to the south nourish stands of thimbleberry, cow-

Bear cable at Horse Creek crossing

parsnip, paintbrush, currant, lupine, goldenrod, meadow rue and swamp whitehead. Near Mosquito Creek the trail drops steeply down to campsites #19 and #20 at the west end of Cold Springs Campground on the East Fork Kaweah River.

Lacking a shuttle here, we walk through the campground past site #6 and climb beside the river on the popular day-use Cold Springs Nature Trail through streamside vegetation. The hiker will notice white-barked aspen trees along this route showing avalanche damage, evidence that perhaps the proposed extensive resort development might not have been the wisest thing for Mineral King Valley. We come out onto the road near the leased summer home sites and return to the start of our journey.

MAIN TRAIL #4

Mineral King to White Chief Meadows
(4 miles one way)

The White Chief Meadows area offers something unusual for the Sierra Nevada—caves. The highest marble caves in the state are found here, and other interesting diversions, such as innumerable marmots, make this a fun trip suitable as a day or an overnight hike. Hikers must be cautioned, however, that exploring these caves can be dangerous (some are on a private inholding as well), and if planning anything more than a cursory peek in, they should

Vandever Mountain and White Chief Peak

contact the rangers at Mineral King Ranger Station for precautions and restrictions.

We start at the Eagle Crest trailhead by the lot west of the river (map section D2) and begin climbing up the west slope above East Fork Kaweah River in sagebrush, juniper, red fir and mountain maple. This maple, a deciduous shrub, and one of the few plants providing fall color here, is identified by its typically 3-lobed maple leaves. We climb to a bridged crossing of Spring Creek, leap over Eagle Creek, and pass the Eagle Lake Trail (Main Trail #5) which heads up to the right.

The going gets steeper beyond the junction, and we can see the Farewell Gap trail below, with Franklin Creek across the canyon. Granitic boulders appear along here — probably erratics left long ago by glaciers — as we pass through mixed open forest of lodgepole, foxtail and silver pine along with red fir. We cross White Chief Creek and skirt White Chief Dry Lake, which was once a lake but now has standing water only early in the year, and a scattering of weathered logs in its bed, dumped by numerous avalanches. Indeed, recent avalanches have not only crossed the lakebed here from west to east, but have actually gone uphill onto the opposite side of the valley.

The stream is increasingly erratic—disappearing and reappearing—because we are now getting into a formation of marble, a metamorphosed form of limestone, which is readily dissolved by water and mild acids in the ground.

Our trail climbs away from the stream and we emerge from timber into grassy meadows carpeted with flowers of gentian, bluebell, yarrow and paintbrush, and overrun by numerous yellow-bellied marmots, which in early season are not only very hungry after a long winter's hibernation, but also have a great curiosity about untended backpacks! We continue upstream another quarter-mile to cross where a shaft has been quarried in the marble above the stream. This tunnel is on a privately owned inholding and may not be explored without the current owners' permission. Check with the rangers in Mineral King for current status of land ownership and spelunking (cave-exploring) restrictions in the White Chief area.

Ducks show us the way up the west wall of the gorge above White Chief Creek, and where we cross, its waters may be only a gurgle underground in late season. After walking a ¼ mile in a meadow where again one will almost surely see marmots, we recross the stream to the west, and soon the trail peters out among marble caves, diggings and rock shelters below what is shown as a pond on the topo map but has since silted in to become a meadow.

From here White Chief Lake is a short cross-country jaunt to the northwest over talus beneath White Chief Peak. Wood is not to be found at the lake, and the few campsites are exposed to the wind. White Chief Peak may easily be climbed from the saddle to the west between this lake and Eagle Lake. In fact, experienced cross-country hikers may want to make a loop trip by climbing to this ridge and walking over to the low pass south of Eagle Lake, descending to the lake, and returning to Mineral King via the Eagle Lake Trail. Also, remote and scenic Ansel Lake may easily be reached from the ridge above the lake or from White Chief Meadows.

MAIN TRAIL #5

Mineral King to Eagle Lake
(3 ½ miles one way)

Dammed about 1904-05 by the Mount Whitney Power and Electric Co., Eagle Lake is still maintained by the Southern California Edison Co. as part of its streamflow-regulation network for power production downstream on the Kaweah River. It's a popular hike for fishing, and anglers who are in good shape can make this a one-day hike.

We take the Eagle Crest Trails route south from

Eagle Lake

Mineral King to the Eagle Lake/Mosquito Lakes turnoff (in map section D2) and on it immediately begin a steep 1/4-mile series of switchbacks up through alternating meadows and timber. The trail levels out somewhat before Eagle Creek Sinkhole, where the stream plunges underground into eroded metamorphic strata, later to reappear above the main trail to these lakes. Our route then climbs away from the creek into a forest of red fir and lodgepole pine as we pass the trail to Mosquito Lakes. (From here the route to Mosquito Lakes climbs steadily through red-fir forest and rounds the nose of Miners Ridge between the Mosquito and Eagle Creek drainages. Then it begins a long, steady *descent* to Mosquito Lake #1, located among dense timber. It yields up catches of eastern brook trout. This lake has seen much overuse, and special regulations are in effect. Campers must stay near the outhouse in the designated area on the west side of the lake, and 100 feet from the shoreline. (The trail beyond Mosquito Lake #1 to the upper lakes is no longer maintained and is not easy to follow. Therefore, it is no longer described in this book.)

Beyond this junction we begin to climb through granite boulders that have weathered from the long ridge between Eagle and Mosquito creeks. Conies are common here, but they are more often heard than seen-—*aack! aack!* After this short, steep stretch, the trail enters open lodgepole back near the stream, and shortly we arrive at the outlet dam of Eagle Lake (10000'). Camping is allowed above the trail, and fishing for eastern brook trout to 8" is good.

From Eagle Lake experienced cross-country hikers may want to try hiking to White Chief, Mosquito or Ansel Lake for interesting off-trail trips.

MAIN TRAIL #6

Mineral King to Big Five Lakes
(16 ½ miles one way)

Although this trip can be done in three or four days by super-hikers, a week should be spent on it to sufficiently savor the beauty of two of the finest groups of lakes in the *Mineral King* quadrangle: the Little and Big Five lakes groups. The route to these lakes may be retraced to make an out-and-back trip. However, a fine loop may be made by coming back to Mineral King via Lost Canyon and Sawtooth Pass (see Main Trail #1).

The trailhead is in Mineral King Valley, at the bend 1 mile above Mineral King Ranger Station (map section D1). For the first ½ mile we are on the Sawtooth Pass Trail (Main Trail #1), which takes off to the right at the first signed fork. Taking the left-hand track, we climb relentlessly upward on this hot, dry, southwest-facing slope. Across Mineral King Valley we note a much denser growth of vegetation on the cooler, moister, northeast-facing slope. Our route passes through scattered patches of juniper and red fir, with flowers of forget-me-not, phlox, lupine, goldenrod and mountain bluebell along the trail. After a steep series of switchbacks, we climb more gently across a sloping meadow and enter a cool stand of red fir, which merges higher up with foxtail pine. In fact, the world's largest known foxtail pine is up here somewhere.

At Timber Gap (signed as 9400') the lowest trail pass out of Mineral King, traces of early mineral exploration have all but succumbed to the elements and nature's decomposing organisms. The trail now drops steeply in red fir and silver pine. During early season in this forest, travelers will hear the thumping of blue grouse and the melodic flutings of hermit thrushes.

As we lose elevation above Timber Gap Creek, active erosion is readily evident in the loosely consolidated metamorphic rocks, and the streams down this slope have a strange habit of disappearing underground, even in early season. Mid-season hikers will be delighted by the luxuriant wildflower gardens along this route. About 2 miles beyond Timber Gap we cross over the ridge on our right and then switchback smoothly down to Cliff Creek in a dense stand of Jeffrey pine, silver pine and white fir. Mule deer and one of their minor predators, the bobcat, might be seen on this trail.

Beyond the ford of Cliff Creek are a fair campsite and a trail junction. Beware of bold bears, and use the food-storage box! Redwood and Bearpaw meadows are downstream to the left (see the High Sierra Hiking Guide to *Triple Divide Peak*), but we head uphill to the right through the camp, towards Black Rock Pass. Our route climbs steadily through alternating patches of brush and stands of trees. Numerous wildflowers dot the path in early season, among them yellow-throated gilia, wallflower, buckwheat, delphinium, Sego lily, rein orchid, wild strawberry and monkeyflower. Beyond a grove of tree-sized willows, our route goes out onto a braided stream channel, and the trail may be lost in the rocks. Just be sure to head for the prominent falls of Cliff Creek, and you will find the trail veering away from the stream and climbing to the left (north) through dense willow, sagebrush, whitethorn and bitter cherry.

Our trail then crosses the outlet from Pinto Lake, and after the next rise we drop down to some meadows beside placid Cliff Creek. There is good camping south of here, though it is mosquitoey in early season. A food-storage box here should be used. We continue across the meadows *without* crossing Cliff Creek, and begin a 3000' ascent up the north wall of Cliff Creek Canyon to Black Rock Pass.

Spring Lake from the Black Rock Pass Trail

There are scattered foxtail pines here, but the slopes are mostly open and the ground cover is a wildflower garden in early season. Especially noticeable are pungent wild onion, streamlined shooting star, golden wallflower and purplish flax.

Higher up, we are able to make out Spring Lake, Cyclamen Lake and Columbine Lake (still ice-covered in early season), in the U-shaped, glacially carved canyon below. Robins are common here, as are the tuneful rock wren and the oft-heard but seldom-seen blue grouse.

At Black Rock Pass (11600') we are in dark metamorphic rock, with the white granite of the Great Western

Two Little 5 Lakes

Divide east and south of us. On a good day we can see all the way to the Mt. Whitney region in the east and the Kaweah Peaks Ridge in the north. Below are both the Big and Little Five Lakes chains.

Late snow often covers the north side of the pass, so we work our way down cautiously, staying to the left of uppermost Little Five Lake, where camping is exposed and wood scarce. The trail re-enters forest cover — lodgepole and foxtail pines — above the second-highest lake. Here good camps can be made around the northern half of the lake. No campfires are allowed above 10400' in the Little Five Lakes basin.

Our trail crosses the outlet of the second-highest lake (a backcountry ranger can be found in the summer on the lake's east side), and just beyond it we come to a signed junction. The trail to the left continues past the lower lakes of the chain before leaving the *Mineral King* quadrangle and dropping toward Big Arroyo (see the High Sierra Hiking Guide to *Triple Divide Peak*). We continue ahead (east) here and travel across rolling terrain in lodgepole forest. Our route contours around the ridge separating the Big and Little Five Lakes drainages, and just over the crest is a fork. (The trail ahead drops on well-graded switchbacks under an open forest of mixed pines to the northeast shore of the lowest of the Big Five Lakes. Good campsites can be made around most of the lake. The route crosses the lake's outlet on rocks and logs and makes a short ascent to a ridge before leveling out past a shallow, unnamed pond on the *Kern Peak* quadrangle. The trail then drops steeply over several benches to a signed junction just before Lost Canyon Creek. Here one can proceed left (southeast) toward Big Arroyo or Soda Creek and Little Claire Lake or one can go right (west) up Lost Canyon toward Columbine Lake and thence to Sawtooth Pass and back to Mineral King — see Main Trails #2 and #1. But we continue on around the ridge to the right (SW) and drop to the north end of the second lake in the chain. Good campsites exist on the shores of this lake.

Continuing on the well-worn trail along the north shore, we come to the outlet and descend it to the longest lake in the chain, Big Five Lake #3. Our route, in wet meadows, skirts the north shore of this lake and climbs its inlet to Lake #4. Early in the season, the fortunate hiker will see golden trout spawning in the clean granite sands of this stream. This lake (#4) has good campsites near the outlet.

The trail becomes less distinct as it continues west along the north side of Lake #4, finally veering away from the lake at the inlet to become a cross-country route toward Glacier Pass. This route is no longer described in this book due to excessive erosion, and its use is not recommended.

MAIN TRAIL #7

Garfield/Hockett Trail--Clough Cave Ranger
Station to Hockett Meadows (12 miles one way)

The lowest-starting trail in the quadrangle, the South Fork Trail climbs about 5000 feet in 12 miles to Hockett Meadows. It's popular with stock parties, while the Ladybug Trail (see Secondary Trail #5), which also starts nearby, is a favorite with families and with those wanting a short hike at low elevations.

The Garfield/Hockett Trail begins at road's end beyond the Clough Cave (South Fork) Campground (just off map section A4 in the *Kaweah* quadrangle). An increasingly rare and disappearing symbol of the American wilderness still exists and is active in the South Fork area--the mountain lion. Sightings are frequent here, and warning signs have been posted for lone hikers to be alert when walking this trail. Mountain lions prey on deer, but the one(s) here is/are becoming habituated to humans and has/have been known to follow hikers. If you should be so fortunate as to have one of these magnificent animals stalk you, do not start running away! It will think *you* are a deer! No attacks have been reported, but be alert so that both we and the lion(s) can continue to enjoy this remnant wild place. The trail soon climbs away from the river in foothill woodland where canyon oak, California bay, incense-cedar and California Torreya are the overstory plants. After weaving in and out of gullies for about 1½ miles, our trail crosses the stream gushing forth from Big Spring, on the *Mineral King* map. As we continue climbing toward Snowslide Canyon (where a rockslide in the winter of 1867 caused a huge flood downstream on the Kaweah River), we get a look across the South Fork to several granite exfoliation domes, including Homer's Nose (see the chapter "Geology").

Our route continues steadily upwards as we enter the Garfield Grove of giant sequoias, which, together with the Dillonwood Grove across Dennison Ridge to the south, makes up what may be the largest continuous stand of sequoias in existence. This grove continues for about three miles along the trail, and its shade and streams make a pleasant task of the steady ascent.

After about 5 ½ miles we pass an obscure, unsigned junction with the unmaintained Summit Lake Trail, which climbs to the right, up through the Garfield Grove to the ridgecrest and eventually meets the Tuohy Creek Trail near Summit Meadow (see Main Trail #8). Beyond this junction we gradually leave the sequoias behind and enter

CAUTION

Mountain
Lion
Habitat

Running and solo hiking in this area are
NOT RECOMMENDED. Children are
particularly vulnerable because of their
small size and their behavior.

Report All Sightings to a Ranger.

Further information at Ranger Stations.

Near Clough Cave Ranger Station

a forest of red firs, where we are likely to see Douglas squirrels busily cutting the cucumber-sized cones of these trees in late season. Then we enter lodgepole-pine forest and pass an obscure trail junction where an abandoned segment of the Old Hockett Trail (also known as the Board Camp Dome Trail) goes off to the left down to the river.

Our trail soon arrives at the South Fork Kaweah River, where crossing can be tricky in high water. After another 0.1 mile we reach a signed junction and a trail register. The trail to Tuohy Meadow and Summit Meadow crosses the river here and goes up Tuohy Creek, eventually meeting the Tuohy Cutoff (see Main Trail #3), and on toward the Summit Lake Trail (Main Trail #8). We go left, however, and after a short climb in open lodgepole come to the short spur that leads left to Hockett Lakes, where quiet camping is assured.

Our route continues ahead another hundred yards to another junction. The trail to the right goes about a mile to meet the Hockett Meadows loop and continues on to South

Fork Meadows (see Main Trail #3). We turn left (N) here and shortly encounter the Hockett Meadows loop at Sand Meadow. From here we follow this trail north another 1½ miles to our destination, Hockett Meadows.

MAIN TRAIL #8

Shake Camp (Mountain Home State Forest) to Summit Lake and Maggie Lakes (25-mile loop trip)

This loop trip gives access to several middle elevation lakes and streams in the Golden Trout Wilderness and to the southern part of Sequoia National Park. After all but the heaviest winters, this route allows entry into the back-country earlier than most of the other trails described in this guide. A wilderness permit is required for this trip, and dogs and firearms are not allowed in the national park.

The trail begins just off the southern edge of the *Mineral King* quadrangle (section B5) in the *Camp Nelson* quadrangle. The trail head is at the entrance to Shake Camp Campground in Mountain Home State Forest and is signed 31E15.

We begin by climbing gently for a few hundred yards through a recently logged forest of white fir, black oak and sugar pine before dropping into the *Mineral King* quad-rangle on a moderate descent to Redwood Crossing on the North Fork of the Middle Fork (or Wishon Fork) of the Tule River. There are several stately giant sequoias here, where a crossing is made during high water on a sequoia log just upstream.

After switchbacking up the east bank, our trail heads north upstream, leaving the Eastside and River trails, which go off to the south. We soon cross the boundary into the Golden Trout Wilderness of Sequoia National Forest, and after a mile of steady climbing, the trail crosses the river and continues up the west bank under red firs. We pass through several wet meadows and soon arrive at a junction with the Frank Knowles Trail, which climbs north (left) for 2-1/2 miles toward Summit Meadow. This trail meets the Cyclone Meadow Trail and the Tuohy Trail, which continues on toward the South Fork of the Kaweah and Hockett Meadows (Main Trails #7 and #3).

We turn right (E) here, continuing on our way to Summit Lake after fording a tributary of the river. The trail next makes a long series of switchbacks in red-fir and then lodgepole-pine forest, climbing almost 2000 feet to Summit Lake, just inside the boundary of Sequoia National Park. The lake is small and well-timbered, with lots of brook trout to be caught.

Our route continues east from the lake, shortly passing the Cyclone Meadow Trail, which goes north, and arrives at another junction. The trail ahead climbs up onto Windy Ridge and meets trails to Blossom Lake and Quinn Patrol Cabin (Main Trail #3 and Secondary Trail #7) at Windy Gap, 2 miles away. Here we turn right (SE) and climb over Sheep Mountain, where we leave the park and re-enter the Golden Trout Wilderness in Sequoia National Forest. From this point south this trail is now known as the Summit

National Recreation Trail.

In upper Peck's Canyon we descend in red-fir forest and arrive at a junction. The trail ahead going down Peck's Canyon passes through private land, and our route has been rerouted around the property. We go right, passing marshy Twin Lakes and Frog Lakes, and eventually arrive at the outlet of lower Maggie Lake. Here we find a heavily used campsite. The other two Maggie Lakes, a short cross-country jaunt away, have limited camping space.

From the outlet of Lower Maggie Lake, we take the ducked trail downstream, pass the obscure and abandoned Hanging Meadow Trail, which goes left to private land, and

Foxtail pines above Little Kern Canyon

continue swinging toward the south, passing a junction with the former Summit Trail.

Climbing, we cross a ridge in red fir and descend to a signed junction with the Griswold Trail, 31E18. We turn right (W) onto this trail and, after a short climb over the south ridge of Maggie Mountain, begin a long, steep, 3700-foot decent to the North Fork of the Middle Fork of the Tule River. Passing through several major vegetation changes on the way, we descend under red fir, then white fir, sugar pine, black oak, incense-cedar and ponderosa pine. Our trail leaves the *Mineral King* quadrangle again to finish up on the *Camp Nelson* map. We re-enter Mountain Home State Forest as the Eastside Fire Trail takes off to the right (N), and just above the river we reach another junction. Here we go right (N) and pass several old mine shafts before crossing Silver Creek to an old cabin. Climbing behind the cabin, our route passes over the next divide to Galena Creek, which is crossed on logs, and then we are once again under the sequoias of Mountain Home State Forest.

Our trail soon crosses the river itself on logs and we pass above a shake-making site before coming to a road just below Moses Gulch Campground. About 10 yards up the road to the right our trail continues climbing uphill on the other side of the road. Then our route switchbacks up about ¼ mile, with a creek to the left, before emerging onto the road again. About 20 yards down toward the stream, the trail continues uphill on the other side. We resume climbing in white fir and sequoias ¼ mile or so to another crossing of the road. Here a sign indicates that we have been climbing the Moses Gulch Trail which resumes again above the road about 100 yards to the left, where a sign says "trail." We continue climbing steeply up the right side of the gully, cross it, and after another steep uphill stretch to the right, come to fire road 30E14. Going right here, we come out in 1/4 mile at the entrance to Shake Camp Campground and trail's end. Good luck! (Detailed maps of the trails in Mountain Home State Forest are available at the Forest headquarters. Also see the Wilderness Press book *Exploring the Southern Sierra*, Vol. 2, by J.C. Jenkins and Ruby Johnson Jenkins.)

SECONDARY TRAIL #1

Atwell Mill to Hockett Meadows
(9 miles one way)

This trail used to be the main northern access to Hockett Meadows, but most hikers now come in from Mineral King trailheads. However, this trail is well-maintained and is a pleasant alternative to the Mineral King route over the Tar Gap Trail. (A car shuttle, hitchhike or 4-mile road walk would be necessary for those starting or ending a Hockett trip on this trail who use Mineral King for the other end of their trek.)

The Atwell/Hockett Trail begins at the lower (west) end of Atwell Mill Campground (map section B1). However, vehicles must be parked at the upper (east) end of the campground, *not* at the trailhead.

Our route heads west in sequoias, black and canyon oaks, incense-cedars and other middle-elevation trees to the remains of Atwell Mill itself, active in the late 1800's when these groves were being logged for grape stakes. At the mill site we turn left and descend to reach the fine bridge over roaring East Fork Kaweah River.

From the river our trail climbs steadily under giant sequoias to Deer Creek, which we cross on stream-slickened granite. A long, steady ascent through mixed forest along with an understory of pungent mountain misery, bracken fern, hazel nut and thimbleberry takes us past vistas of the lower canyon and the Central Valley, and into and out of the drainages of Clover and Corner creeks before arriving at a signed junction and a trail register. The trail to the left (N) leads to Mineral King via the Tar Gap Trail, but we turn right (S). Our route now follows the Hockett Meadows Trail (Main Trail #3) for two miles to Hockett Meadows, where our journey ends.

SECONDARY TRAIL #2

Atwell Mill to Paradise Peak (4 miles one way)

For those wanting a brief introduction to the lower-elevation forests of Mineral King with a fantastic view thrown in, this is *the* trail. Hikers interested in an alternative, uncrowded route to the Giant Forest from Mineral King may also want to consider taking this trail to the Redwood Meadow turnoff and continuing north from there.

The trail starts about ¼ mile west of the entrance to Atwell Mill Campground (map section B1) on the Mineral King road, and it is signed for Paradise Ridge and Redwood Meadow. We immediately begin a long 2900-foot ascent in a mixed forest of sequoia, white fir and sugar pine.

Numerous wildflowers including lupines, wallflowers and monkeyflowers delight the nose and eye as we proceed upward on long switchbacks under some fine giant sequoias—spared the woodsmen's ax with the establishment of Sequoia National Park in 1890. About 2½ miles of steady climbing, by now into mountain chaparral, bring us to the crest of the divide.

The trail ahead (N) to Redwood Meadow is described from the edge of the map in the High Sierra Hiking Guide to *Triple Divide Peak*. We head west up the ridge for about two miles, mainly on the crest under a sparse cover of red fir and silver pine, the trail littered with deadfall, till we arrive at Paradise Peak (9362'), where there is, somewhat obtrusively, a Park Service radio repeater. Nonetheless, it's a great spot to gaze about and enjoy lunch, with superb views in all directions: the Central Valley to the west, Castle Rocks to the north and the Great Western Divide to the east. And it's all downhill going back!

SECONDARY TRAIL #3

Hockett Meadows Trail to Rattlesnake Creek
(6 miles)

This lateral trail goes up Shotgun Creek, past Silver Lake, and over Shotgun Pass to Rattlesnake Creek, connecting the Hockett Meadows Trail (Main Trail #3) with the Franklin Pass Trail (Main Trail #2). Hikers may wish to use this lateral to make a loop trip from Mineral King over Farewell Gap, returning via Franklin Pass.

At either of two successive forks, more or less across the Little Kern from Broder's Cabin (map sections D3 and E3), this route leaves the Hockett Meadows Trail and heads southeast across loose, mostly unshaded metamorphic rocks. The upper, more level fork, unmaintained and washed out in spots, joins the second, lower fork, which is switchbacked and more recently maintained, and this combined trail crosses the ridge dotted with red fir and Jeffrey pine. The trail passes an abandoned trail to the right that continues as the Lion Meadows Trail (Secondary Trail #6), and descends through chaparral towards Shotgun Creek. At the partially signed junction just before the creek, the Coyote Trail ahead begins a steady climb in pine and fir and soon passes a cutoff that drops to the right (the Lion Meadows Trail). The Coyote Trail continues generally upward in and out of the drainages of Pistol and Rifle creeks on granite sand until it leaves the *Mineral King* quadrangle.

Back at Shotgun Creek we turn left onto the unsigned trail to Silver Lake and switchback steeply up the west bank of Shotgun Creek through mountain chaparral. This trail *has* to be more fun going down than going up. The trail is loose and dusty underfoot, but soon passes into the welcome shade of lodgepole pine and red fir. Gradually the gradient lessens as we climb out into meadows dotted with willow scrub and numerous wildflowers, especially colorful in midseason. The trail stays high, well west of the creek, before beginning a series of switchbacks in foxtail pine which bring us to Silver Lake (10500' +). Silver Lake is a medium-sized tarn surrounded by granite ridges. Camping is scenic, and the sandy beach on the east side makes for ideal swimming in mid- and late season.

Silver Lake from the Shotgun Pass Trail

Our trail crosses the lake's outlet and climbs rather obscurely up the granite-sand slope east of the lake. We soon break out of foxtail-pine forest onto open slopes, and switchback to the easy summit (11400') of Shotgun Pass. From the pass we can see all the way to the Sierra Crest near Mt. Whitney; closer are the Kern Trench, Rattlesnake Canyon and, to the north, Kaweah Peaks Ridge; Florence Peak and Franklin Pass are nearer yet. The unofficial trail down the north side of the pass into Sequoia National Park (no pets or firearms permitted) is ducked as it descends toward Rattlesnake Creek in granite grus, over slabs and around boulders. Occasionally, we can see where soil is forming alongside rocks as plants establish themselves in their rather harsh environment — a stage in the process of ecological succession.

Next, we cross a wet meadow to the directly opposite edge and follow ducks and triangular blazes as we enter lodgepole cover. It is easy to lose the route here. Hikers who can follow the blazes and are able to stay on the route will reach Rattlesnake Creek at a signed junction with the Franklin Pass (Rattlesnake Creek) Trail. Even if you lose the route somewhere along here, it's possible to merely continue downhill, heading north, and reach Rattlesnake Creek. In either case, the hiker will intersect the Franklin Pass Trail (perhaps at the signed junction) after crossing the creek, and most likely at a point west of the fork where the trails to Little Claire Lake and lower Rattlesnake Creek diverge (see Main Trail #2).

SECONDARY TRAIL #4

Hockett Meadows to Evelyn Lake
and Cahoon Rock (2 ½ miles each, one way)

Evelyn Lake offers hikers taking the Hockett Meadows Trail something special along this stretch of the trail: a lake that is more a lake than a marsh. Blossom Lakes and Hockett Lakes, described along the Hockett Meadows Trail (Main Trail #3), have undergone ecological succession to the point that they are mostly muck-bottomed and may freeze solid during the winter, thus killing any fish. Evelyn Lake is still fairly deep, and it offers both swimming (in late season) and good fishing (in early season).

To get there, we take the signed trail just north of Hockett Meadows Ranger Station (map section B3) and head west past a campsite along Whitman Creek. In less than a mile we ford Whitman Creek and continue ahead. Climbing under red fir, we cross Cow Creek (not shown on the topo map) and come to another fork. The trail ahead goes to Cahoon Rock, which can be reached in less than a mile of climbing through several flower-filled wet meadows. The lookout tower is gone, but good views can still be had to Dennison Ridge, the Central Valley and to the Great Western Divide. At the fork we turn north toward Evelyn Lake, soon topping a ridge between the valleys of Cahoon Creek and Whitman Creek. Golden-mantled ground squirrels are abundant here, and one can distinguish them from chipmunks by their large size, lack of facial striping, and yellowish head.

We continue along the ridgetop for less than a mile and then begin dropping steeply to the west, toward Evelyn Lake. Pinedrops, a nonphotosynthesizing flowering plant, is common here under the pine and fir. At Evelyn Lake camping is best where the trail comes in; it's also good across the lake in a stand of trees on the west side.

SECONDARY TRAIL #5

South Fork Trail to Ladybug and Whiskey Log Camps (4 miles one way)

The Ladybug Trail is the most popular hike from Clough Cave (South Fork) Campground and affords the gentlest introduction to backpacking in the Mineral King area. And it is open year-round. Hikers in this area are cautioned to be alert for several potential hazards. The first is the river itself. Especially in early season, and any time of the summer after a very snowy winter, stream flows can be swift and cold, and water-smoothed boulders in the river can be very slippery. Drownings are possible, and they have occurred here. Second, a mountain lion (or lions) is active in this area and is becoming habituated to hikers. Don't let children wander alone around here. Hikers finding themselves being followed by a mountain lion should *not* run, as the lion could perceive them as prey. Third, and probably most important as a potential hazard here, is poison-oak.

This plant is an abundant shrub/vine along the South Fork, and if you go here, you should first learn to recognize it. Most of the year this plant can be identified by its three oak-like leaflets, with wavy margins. Unfortunately it can cause a skin rash any time of the year, even when leafless in the winter. Avoid touching this plant at any time.

We start at the end of the road a short distance beyond the Campground (just west of map section A4, in the *Kaweah* quadrangle) and drop to a bridged crossing of the river. In a few hundred yards, a short spur trail leads up to Clough Cave, which unfortunately has been heavily vandalized due to its easy access, and is closed to the public most of the year. However, in recent years, it has been open (contact the Clough Cave Ranger Station for permission and key) during August when an endangered species of bat that spends most of the year in the cave leaves for awhile. In addition, there are at least six endemic species of spiders in Clough Cave. This is a special place! So, should you visit, tread lightly. Other caves in this area require special skills and permission; check with Park staff for more information.

Our route stays above the river several hundred feet in a dense cover of oaks for a mile before turning north to ford Squaw Creek, the first water since the river crossing. In another ¾ mile we veer right at a trail fork and arrive at Ladybug Camp on the South Fork — a popular local camping site. It's named, of course, for large masses of ladybird beetles ("ladybugs") which often congregate near here. Thirty-foot Ladybug Falls in just downstream from the campsite. Pools in the river here offer fine opportunities for dipping. However, going into the water could be fatal when the river is high, in early to mid season.

The trail continues through the campsite and rejoins the main route upcanyon after a short switchback in ponderosa pine and incense-cedar. We climb high above the South Fork, entering a dense stand of incense-cedar and dropping to a ford of Cedar Creek, under the shade of giant sequoias. Camping is no longer permitted here, to protect the trees.

Beyond Cedar Creek, the trail climbs up the ridge to the east and passes an abandoned trail to the left toward Cahoon Rock. After another ¾ mile of climbing above the river, the trail drops down to the water's edge at Whiskey Log Camp. Past this campsite, the trail soon becomes overgrown and difficult to follow, so we end our hike here.

SECONDARY TRAIL #6

Hockett Meadows Loop to Lion Meadows
via Little Kern River (9 miles one way)

For those interested in visiting lower parts of the Little Kern River in the Golden Trout Wilderness, this trail leads from the Hockett Meadows Loop (Main Trail #3) south to Lion Meadows and Grey Meadow. Connections from this route can be made to trails heading east into the *Kern Peaks* quadrangle as well.

We leave the Hockett Meadows Loop Trail a mile before it crosses the Little Kern River south of Farewell

Gap (map section D3 or E3) and continue south along the Shotgun Pass Lateral (Secondary Trail #3) to a divide 3/4 mile before Shotgun Creek. Here there's an abandoned, unsigned trail heading downhill to the right, and we take it to a lower crossing of Shotgun Creek. Soon after jumping across Shotgun Creek we meet the "official" trail coming down from the Coyote Trail above (again refer to Secondary Trail #3) and continue dropping through open Jeffrey pine, white and red fir, and montane chaparral to Pistol Creek. We next cross a low divide to a signed crossing of Rifle Creek, after which our trail soon forks and we head left (S) toward Lion Meadows.

Kaweah Peaks Ridge from Little 5 Lakes

(To the right is *Rifle Creek Public Area*, where the Little Kern Trail (intermittently maintained) crosses Rifle Creek and heads northwest beside the river; several nice campsites exist along this stretch of trail. After a two-mile ascent in chaparral this trail fords the river at benchmark 7923. The trail then climbs beside Wet Meadows Creek to a junction with Secondary Trail #7, which connects the Hockett Meadows Loop to Quinn Patrol Cabin.)

Continuing on the trail towards Lion Meadows, we pass an obscure junction with a cutoff going back northwest to the *Rifle Creek Public Area* and soon arrive at what is signed, *Rifle Creek Public Campground and Corrals*, where there is an established packer campsite. Dropping steadily from here in pine and fir mixed with some western juniper, we stroll above the river, cross a small, unnamed stream and reach fenced Tamarack Meadow at Tamarack Creek. The fortunate hiker may see the lovely yellow, red and black male western tanager here catching insects in his sallies over the meadow.

Leaving Tamarack Creek, our granite-sand trail climbs another low ridge and then gradually descends to Willow Creek and a signed junction with the Coyote Lakes Trail (32E04) – or Hunters Trail – which heads east, uphill out of the quadrangle.

Shortly after crossing Willow Creek, our route leaves the *Mineral King* quadrangle and enters *Kern Peak*. We cross a fork of Willow Creek and several obscure trail junctions before arriving at Lion Meadows, where there's a private boys' camp and fenced pastures. Cattle are still grazed in this area, so be sure to close all gates behind you along the trail. (From just north of Lion Meadows the Nelson Cabin Trail, 32E08 on the topo map, heads west about two miles, crossing the Little Kern and meeting Secondary Trail #7.)

Our trail continues southeast out of Lion Meadows, briefly re-enters the *Mineral King* quadrangle at Table Meadow Creek, and then leaves the map for good, passing into the *Camp Nelson* quadrangle. There it crosses the Little Kern above its confluences with Alpine Creek and Sagebrush Gulch before continuing on to eventually join up with the Clicks Creek Trail coming in from the south, a mile before Grey Meadow. See Secondary Trail #7 for a description of the route between this junction and Quinn Patrol Cabin.

SECONDARY TRAIL #7

Hockett Meadows Loop to Quinn Patrol Cabin and Alpine Creek (12 miles one way)

Portions of this route follow an infrequently maintained and sometimes hard-to-find trail in the Golden Trout Wilderness that connects the Hockett Meadows Trail with Alpine and Mountaineer creeks in the vicinity of the Little Kern River. It does offer experienced pathfinders a possible loop trip in the Little Kern drainage when used in conjunction with the trail to Lion Meadows (Secondary Trail #6). However, most visitors to this area come in from trailheads south of *Mineral King* quadrangle, and the

Wilderness Press book *Exploring the Southern Sierra*, Vol. 2 covers these routes.

This trail heads south from the Hockett Meadows Loop (Main Trail #3) at a signed junction east of Wet Meadows (map section D3). In ½ mile it soon branches right (SW) from a trail that heads northeast to the Little Kern River (see Secondary Trail #6) and contours southwest in red- and white-fir forest to soon enter Sequoia National Park and drop into the meadows at Quinn Patrol Cabin, manned irregularly by Park Service rangers.

A somewhat dank camp can be made in the lodgepole pines across the creek flowing from the meadow. Through the trees a trail climbs west uphill 1½ miles to Windy Gap (9679'). From Windy Gap trails head south to Summit and Maggie lakes and north to the Hockett Trail (Main Trails #8 and #3).

However, we head south from Quinn Cabin and soon reach Upper Soda Spring Creek, which we follow downstream before crossing it to re-enter the Golden Trout Wilderness. From here the trail (labelled Old Hockett Trail, 31E23, on the Sequoia National Forest map) has not recently been maintained for about the first mile, and only experienced trail-finders should attempt the route. It is heavily overgrown with whitethorn and fir and incense-cedar reproduction. Blazes and cut logs, as well as other evidence of a trail, do exist, and those with a good nose for trail location may find their way to the recently reopened section above Walker's Cabin. The cabin and nearby flower-filled meadow seem to be a favorite campsite for Boy Scouts (judging by the profuse graffiti), but we continue on, crossing the meadow and descending through mixed conifer forest on a now-evident trail. We soon pass the signed site of Nelson Cabin and reach two junctions at Lower Soda Spring Creek, across which and heading east is the Nelson Cabin Trail (32E08) to Lion Meadows (see Secondary Trail #6).

From this junction we continue *south* over a low ridge, and leave the *Mineral King* quadrangle to enter *Camp Nelson*, drop slightly in Jeffrey pine past a series of obscure junctions, and finally veer right to ford Alpine Creek. Near the large meadow here is a popular campsite for youth groups.

Once across Alpine Creek the trail rounds a low point and crosses granite-bound Mountaineer Creek, which is blessed with numerous fine campsites downstream from the crossing. After following the south bank of Mountaineer Creek for about 1/3 mile, the trail cuts southward away from the stream though cattle-grazed Jeffrey-pine forest to eventually join the trail from Lion Meadows (32E11) (Secondary Trail #6) a mile above Grey Meadow. A loop hike could be made from here north, or one could branch south, east or west (see *Exploring the Southern Sierra*, Vol. 2).

SELECTED REFERENCES

Adler, Pat, *Mineral King Guide*. Glendale, California: La Siesta Press, 1975.

Albright, Horace Marden and Marian Albright Schenck, *The Mather Mountain Party of 1915*. Three Rivers, California: Sequoia Natural History Association, no date.

Brown, Henry McLauren, *Mineral King Country, Visalia to Mount Whitney*. Fresno: Pioneer Publishing, 1988.

Dilsaver, Lary M. and William C. Tweed, *Challenge of the Big Trees*. Three Rivers, California: Sequoia Natural History Association, 1990.

Elsasser, A.B., *Indians of Sequoia and Kings Canyon National Parks*. Three Rivers, California: Sequoia Natural History Association, 1988.

Farquhar, Francis P., *History of the Sierra Nevada*. Berkeley: U.C. Press, 1959.

Flint, Wendell D., *To Find the Biggest Tree*. Three Rivers, California: Sequoia Natural History Association, 1987.

Gerstenberg, R.H., *Common Trees and Shrubs of the Southern Sierra Nevada*. R.H. Gerstenberg, 1983.

Graydon, Don, ed., *Mountaineering, the Freedom of the Hills*. Seattle: The Mountaineers, 1992.

Hartsveldt, Richard J., et al., *Giant Sequoias*. Three Rivers, California: Sequoia Natural History Association, 1981.

Jackson, Louise A., *Beulah, A Biography of the Mineral King Valley of California*. Tucson: Westernlore Press, 1988.

McMinn, Howard E. and Evelyn Maino, *Pacific Coast Trees*. Berkeley: U.C. Press, 1959.

National Geographic Society, *Field Guide to Birds of North America*. Washington, D.C., 1987.

Peterson, Roger Tory, *A Field Guide to Western Birds*. Boston: Houghton, 1990.

Sorenson, Steve, *Day Hiking Sequoia*. Three Rivers, California: Manzanita Press, 1991.

Storer, Tracy I. and Robert L. Usinger, *Sierra Nevada Natural History*. Berkeley: U.C. Press, 1963.

Strong, Douglas Hillman, Trees . . . or Timber? *The Story of Sequoia and King Canyon National Parks*. Three Rivers, California: Sequoia Natural History Association, 1986.

Tweed, William C., and Lary M. Dilsaver, *Sequoia Yesterdays, Centennial Photo History*. Three Rivers, California: Sequoia Natural History Association, Inc., 1990.

United States Department of Agriculture, Forest Service, *Map of Sequoia National Forest*. Washington, D.C., 1990.

U.S. Depart. of the Interior, National Park Service, *Environmental Assessment, Comprehensive Management Plan, Sequoia and Kings Canyon National Parks--Mineral King*, 1980.

Whitney, Stephen, *A Sierra Club Naturalist's Guide to the Sierra Nevada*. San Francisco: Sierra Club, 1979.

Index

Index

1996 Update

Page 36: Mineral King rangers recommend bringing enough chicken wire to completely encircle the undercarriage of your vehicle (hold in place with rocks) to prevent marmot damage in early season.

Page 37: The first Mineral King parking lot is about 0.3 mile above the ranger station and is signed as the "Tar Gap" parking area.

Page 37: Due to federal budget cuts, the ranger station at the Clough Cave Campground no longer exists. The campground may be staffed by volunteer campground "hosts" during the summer (bless 'em!). (Note: there is no gasoline at South Fork.)

Pages 37–38: Expanded directions to Shake Camp in Mountain Home State Forest and the Summit and Maggie Lakes Trailhead: Get onto state highway 190 just south of Porterville and take it northeast through Springville. One mile east of Springville, turn north (left) onto Balch Park Road (J37/MTN 239). In about 3½ miles turn east (right) onto Bear Creek Road (MTN 220). Reach Mountain Home State Forest in about 14 miles on the steep, winding road, passing the turnoff (left) to the headquarters. Continue straight ahead and in a little over a mile, turn right at the next junction (signed). In about 3½ miles reach Shake Camp Campground. The trailhead and parking are at the entrance to the campground (where camping is free).

Page 40: Federal budget cuts have greatly curtailed trail maintenance in the Golden Trout Wilderness. Hikers are advised to inquire about trail conditions here in advance at the Forest Service offices listed above.

Page 41, Main Trail #1: The first mile passes through a prescribed natural burn from 1994. Note the regrowth of grasses here, which have come in to replace the once dominant shrubs, such as sagebrush. This is an example of a process known to ecologists as secondary succession.

Page 42, Main Trail #1: The first fork is less than a mile up the trail.

Page 57: Camping is no longer permitted between the trail and Whitman Creek at Hockett Meadows.

Page 59, Main Trail #3: The Hockett Meadows Loop Trail enters Cold Springs Campground near campsite #19 and the walk-in campsites.

Page 64: Camping is no longer allowed at Mosquito Lake #1.

Page 65, Main Trail #6: For less than a mile at the start we are on the Sawtooth Pass Trail.

Page 70, Main Trail #7: This trail starts at the South Fork Campground, just before road's end. Also, mountain lions have **not** recently been seen in this area (1996).

Page 72: This pictured mountain-lion warning notice is no longer current.

Page 74: Note that the sequoia log upstream over Redwood Creek can be slippery if wet.

Page 76: The Griswold Trail (31E18) was strewn with wind-throw in 1996.

Page 76: The shake-making site below Moses Gulch Camp-ground is no longer obvious.

Page 77: The trail forks left off of Fire Road 30E14 about 150 yards before reaching the Shake Camp trailhead and parking area.

Page 79: The trail along the ridge to Paradise Peak is no longer maintained.

Page 84, Secondary Trail #5: The campground is now designated as the South Fork Campground. Mountain lions have **not** been seen here recently (1996).

Page 85: The Clough Cave Ranger Station no longer exists. Prospective spelunkers must inquire at Park Headquarters, Ash Mountain, regarding access to Clough Cave.

Page 94: *Exploring the Southern Sierra, vol. 2* was published in 1992. The present edition of *Sierra South* is 1993. The present edition of *Backpacking Basics* is 1994.